Behavioral Arbitrage

Behavioral Arbitrage

Why the most profitable acts are the ones no one dares to do

Gabriel Toledo

Behavioral Arbitrage
Why the most profitable acts are the ones no one dares to do

First edition: 2026

The thesis, the structure, and the editorial decisions of this book are the author's. The text was written with the assistance of artificial intelligence, and this English edition was translated and adapted from the Spanish original with the same assistance.

Originally published in Spanish as Arbitraje conductual (2026).

ISBN: 979-8-9971307-2-5

Cover design: Gabriel Toledo
Cover photograph: Rania Brahim, 2026
Good Life Creations
goodlifecreations.org · info@goodlifecreations.org

For my parents, who gave me the freedom to create and made my world infinite.

Contents

Prologue

This book was written with the assistance of Claude, the artificial intelligence made by Anthropic, and this English edition was translated and adapted from the Spanish with that same assistance. I want to say so here, before the argument begins, because avoiding it would contradict everything the book defends.

I am Gabriel Toledo, a finance student, and I am twenty years old. The idea of this book is mine; it came to me during a semester of personal challenges, and I worked on it until I found its thesis, its cracks, its arguments for and against. The decisions are mine too: what goes in and what gets cut, how it is ordered, the design and the structure. What is not mine is the writing of each sentence—that I built with the AI. I first wrote the book in Spanish, my own language, and this English version was carried over with the same help, keeping the ideas and the decisions mine while the phrasing was rebuilt to read as if it had been written in English from the start. I would rather say all of this plainly, and so acknowledge and value what was shared work.

I know some will see a lesser merit in this, because I did not directly write each word. I see it differently. That a university student can take an idea of their own, refine it over months, and carry it all the way to a finished book does not strike me as a shortcut; it strikes me as a revolution in the way we create. The barrier that separated having an idea from turning it into a work has just come down for everyone, and this book is, more than anything, proof of that.

That is my wish for these pages: not only to defend a thesis about why almost no one does what they could, but to show it with the book itself. We live in a time when anyone with an idea and something to say can, this very day, begin. The ability to create is within reach.

PART I

The Discovery

Chapter 1. The Silent Car

There are acts of negligible cost and high benefit that almost no one performs.

Picture a subway car at rush hour. Thirty people packed into a few square meters, closer to one another than they would ever choose to be, and nearly all of them with their eyes sunk into a screen. No one speaks. Whoever has no phone at hand studies the floor, or the ceiling, or the middle distance, with the deliberate care of someone avoiding another person's eyes. Between them all they have built, without ever agreeing to it, a pact of silence as firm as if it were written down.

This is not a scene. It is a natural experiment, and its virtue is that it repeats itself identically thousands of times a day, in every city in the world, with enormous samples and stable conditions. What can be observed in that car—precisely because it can always be observed—is not an anecdote but a piece of data. And the data is this: in a space full of people, the amount of human contact anyone initiates tends toward zero, not out of physical impossibility—they are a foot apart—but out of something we have not yet named, and that this entire book sets out to name.

Now introduce a single variation. One person, just one, breaks the pact. She says something to whoever is beside her: a remark about the delay, a question about a station, anything at all. It is worth looking coldly at what has just happened, because that minimal act contains the structure of everything that follows.

What it costs and what it might return

The first thing to measure is the cost, and the cost is surprisingly small. In the worst case, that person gets a curt reply, a puzzled look, or the uncomfortable silence of someone who did not want to be interrupted. That is all. The discomfort it produces is real, but it is of a very particular kind: it is brief—measured in seconds; it is bounded—its ceiling is absurdly low, no one has ever died or lost anything tangible over a snub on the train; and it is private—the other passengers forget it before they reach their stop, if they notice it at all. The cost, measured without the distortion that the fear of paying it adds, is almost negligible.

The second thing to measure is what that act might return, and here the arithmetic turns interesting, because the range is enormous. The vast majority of the time, nothing: a courteous exchange that dies in two sentences and is forgotten. But not always. Sometimes the conversation reveals a shared interest, and a connection comes of it. Sometimes that connection turns out to be someone who works at the place you have been trying to get into. Sometimes it is the beginning of a twenty-year friendship, or a marriage, or an idea that rearranges a life. It usually does not happen. But it can, and when it does, the return is of an order that bears no proportion whatsoever to the price paid.

Hold on to the shape of this arithmetic, because it is the shape of the whole book: a small cost, known and bounded, on one side; on the other, a benefit that is almost always nothing but that once in a while is immense. I am not yet claiming why that shape is so favorable—that requires machinery I will build later, carefully, because it is the part that holds up everything else. For now it is enough to see it and accept it as an observable fact: the person who spoke in the car bought, for almost nothing, an open possibility. And the other twenty-nine did not buy it.

One car among thousands of cars

It would be a mistake to think this is about subways, or about talking to strangers. The car is only the cleanest case, the one that best isolates the variable, but the same pattern shows up everywhere once you learn to recognize it.

It is in the person who has a question in a crowded room and does not ask it, afraid of looking foolish, while half the room had the same doubt and would have silently thanked her. It is in the person who admires someone and never says so, keeping to himself a compliment that costs nothing and would have made the other's day. It is in the person who needs help and does not ask, pricing in a rejection that almost never arrives in the magnitude he fears. It is in the person who writes something and does not publish it, in the one who has an idea for a project and never sends the first email, in the one who would like to reconnect with an old friend and lets another year slip by, and then another. In every one of these cases the structure is the same as the car's: an act available to anyone, trivial in cost, with a possible benefit ranging from nothing to enormous, and which the overwhelming majority of people do not perform.

It is an entire class of acts, not a list of tricks. And what they have in common is not the subject—speaking, asking, publishing, thanking bear no resemblance to one another—but the profile: cheap to do, open-ended in what it might return, and systematically avoided.

The anomaly

And this is where the thing becomes a problem, not just an observation. Because if these acts are so cheap and their possible benefit so high, then they represent, in the language I will use throughout the book, an excess return available at almost no cost. A good deal in plain sight of everyone.

What we know about any system populated by people pursuing, however clumsily, their own advantage, is that good deals in plain sight do not last. As soon as an opportunity appears and becomes visible, someone takes it, and then someone else, and the very fact of their taking it closes it, until it stops being an opportunity. Easy returns are exhausted by competition. It is the most basic intuition about how a market behaves, and you do not need to be an economist to have it: if there really were easy money lying there, it would already be gone, because someone would have taken it.

That is why what we observe in the car is an anomaly in the precise sense of the word: a persistent deviation from what an efficient system ought to produce. The opportunity is there, it is good, it is visible, anyone could take it, and yet it is not exhausted. It stays available, car after car, day after day, generation after generation. Twenty-nine people out of thirty let it pass, and they will let it pass tomorrow, and the day after. The good deal in plain sight has not only failed to close: it gives not the faintest sign of ever closing.

Something in this arithmetic does not add up. A return this accessible should not survive the competition of billions of people who supposedly want things to go well for them. That it survives—that it has been surviving for the whole of human history—is the central puzzle of this book, and it is not solved by shrugging or by calling it shyness. It has a structure, and the structure has an explanation.

The first step toward explaining it is to name it precisely, because everything that can be said afterward depends on the precision of the name. What we have been describing—a persistent good deal that no one takes—has an exact name in the vocabulary of finance, and that name is the subject of the next chapter.

Chapter 2. Money on the Ground

It is an arbitrage, but on human behavior.

There is an old joke among economists. Two of them are walking down the street when one spots a twenty on the ground. He bends to pick it up, and the other stops him: "Don't bother. If it were real, someone would have picked it up already." The joke is told to mock a certain blind faith in the efficiency of markets, but it is worth taking seriously for a moment, because it holds a truth and, alongside it, the exact error this book means to dismantle.

The truth is this: in a market with many attentive participants, obvious opportunities for riskless gain do not last. If a stock can be bought cheap in one place and sold dear in another at the same instant, someone will do it, and in doing so will push the cheap price up and the dear one down, until the gap closes and the profit vanishes. That operation—exploiting a single mispriced asset to pocket the difference without exposure—is called arbitrage. And its defining trait, the one to burn into memory, is that arbitrage destroys itself. It exists only until it is discovered; the moment it is discovered, the very act of exploiting it erases it. That is why the skeptical economist is, on his own turf, very nearly right: in a liquid, competitive market, the twenty on the ground is a rarity that lasts seconds, because a thousand hands are ready to bend down.

This book is about a twenty that has been lying on the ground for the whole of human history, and that no one bends down for.

What it is and what it is not

It is worth being honest about the term, because a finance person will object, and will be partly right. Arbitrage in the strict sense is risk-free: a certain gain, with no possibility of loss. The acts I am talking about are not that. Speaking to a stranger can go badly; rejection is a possible outcome, not an impossible one. Strictly, then, we are not looking at pure arbitrage but at something slightly different: a persistent anomaly, a positive expected return that survives where it should not, more kin to those inefficiencies markets never quite correct than to the literal bill on the pavement.

But the imprecision, looked at closely, does not weaken the analogy: it sharpens it. What is essential to arbitrage—what makes the image of the bill on the ground the right one—is not so much the total absence of risk as the scandalous disproportion between what is risked and what can be gained, added to the persistence of the opportunity despite being in plain sight of everyone. And that disproportion is present, in its most extreme form. What is risked is a few seconds of discomfort; what can be gained has no ceiling. The risk exists, but it is so bounded and the expected return so favorable that, for practical purposes, the thing behaves like an arbitrage: money on the ground that competition should have swept up centuries ago and did not. To call it behavioral arbitrage is not to exaggerate; it is to point out that we are looking at the same creature—a good deal that is destroyed on being taken—but in a market that, for some reason, refuses to take it.

With the precision made, I keep using the word, because no other captures so well the image that matters: the dropped bill, visible, real, and the hands that do not move.

An arbitrage open for centuries

Here is the fact that ought to keep us up at night. In financial markets, alpha—excess return, the edge over what the average delivers—is scarce and short-lived by nature. A strategy that works attracts imitators; the imitators exploit it; the exploitation exhausts it. Professionals even have a name for the phenomenon: alpha decay. Every edge, however good, degrades over time as more people discover and use it, until it becomes indistinguishable from the average. The useful life of a good investment idea is measured in months, sometimes weeks. The market is a machine that devours its own opportunities.

Behavioral arbitrage defies that law entirely. It has been open for as long as human beings have existed, and shows not the slightest decay. The twenty was on the ground of the Athenian agora and it is on the ground of the subway car today. The people who dare to speak, to ask, to publish, to approach, remain as rare and go on gaining an advantage as disproportionate now as a thousand years ago. The opportunity has not been exhausted by competition, is not being exhausted, and gives no sign that it ever will be. It is, in the landscape of human opportunities, something almost impossible: a source of advantage that does not run dry.

And it is worth noticing just how strange this is, because the strangeness is the clue. If a seam of gold were discovered tomorrow at ground level, in a public square, free to anyone who bent down, it would not last a morning: it would fill with people, and within hours not a nugget would remain. That is how valuable, accessible resources behave. This one does not behave that way. This one has spent millennia at ground level, free, in the public square, and remains almost untouched. The advantage that comes from daring does not dilute no matter how many dare, because the few remain few, always, in every era.

The real question

So the question is no longer whether there is money on the ground. There is; the previous chapter established it and this one gave it a name. Nor is it whether it is worth picking up, which the chapters on the mechanics will prove with rigor. The real question, the only one that truly matters and the one that organizes everything that comes next, is another, and it is exactly the one the skeptical economist took as answered without examining it: if the bill were real, wouldn't someone have picked it up already?

In markets, the answer is yes, and that is why the joke works. In human behavior, the answer is no, and that is why the joke, applied here, becomes profoundly wrong. The bill is real—it is worth a great deal—and yet no one picks it up, decade after decade, century after century. An arbitrage that does not close is a contradiction in terms for anyone who understands how markets work. That this one exists, and is permanent, is not a curious detail: it is a signal. A good deal that no one takes across all of history is saying something, at the top of its voice, about the nature of the barrier that prevents its being taken. Because a barrier capable of stopping the entire species, without exception and without wear, generation after generation, cannot be an ordinary barrier.

Finding out what that barrier is made of—why, against all market logic, the money stays on the ground—is the task of the next chapter. And the answer begins by ruling out the most obvious explanation, which also turns out to be the wrong one: that the bill is still there is not, as one might think, because bending down is hard.

Chapter 3. Why Nobody Bends Down

It is not difficulty: anyone can bend down. It is courage, and because the barrier is universal, the arbitrage never closes.

An arbitrage that does not close demands an explanation, because it contradicts everything we know about how opportunities behave when there are people around who want to seize them. In real markets, when an inefficiency persists, there is always a reason, and the reason is almost never that no one sees it. It is that capturing it turns out, for some concrete reason, to be hard. You need a great deal of capital for the operation to be worthwhile. You need speed, infrastructure, inside information, a license, a permit. The twenty is on the ground, yes, but behind a pane of glass that costs nineteen to break. Those reasons—the real costs and obstacles that prevent exploiting a visible opportunity—are what specialists call the limits of arbitrage, and they are the standard explanation for why some bargains survive.

The bargain is real, but picking it up is expensive, or slow, or risky in a way that does not pay.

The temptation is to explain our behavioral arbitrage the same way: the bill is still on the ground because bending down is, at bottom, hard. It is a comfortable explanation and it is false, and showing that it is false is the indispensable first step, because only when the easy answer is discarded does the true one appear.

Bending down is not hard

Consider what picking up this bill actually requires. To speak to a stranger you need no capital: it is free. You need no speed and no infrastructure: it is done with your mouth, standing up, without tools. You need no inside information, no license, no permit, no years of training. You need no talent; it is not a scarce skill that some possess and others do not, like playing the violin or solving equations. A five-year-old knows how to do it, and in fact does it effortlessly, until he learns not to. The means to capture this opportunity are distributed perfectly and universally: everyone, without exception, already holds them, complete, from the start and at no cost.

This is exactly the opposite of what happens with the classic limits of arbitrage. There, the barrier is in the world: the capital you do not have, the speed you cannot reach, the glass you cannot break. Here there is no glass. There is no external barrier at all. The bill is on the ground, bare, with nothing on top of it, and bending down costs not a cent and requires no capacity the person does not already possess.

And yet no one bends down. Which, far from resolving the puzzle, sharpens it to the point of near-unbearableness. Because if the opportunity is good and capturing it demands nothing people do not have, then the barrier cannot be in the world. It has to be somewhere else. It has to be inside.

The barrier is inside, and that is why it does not yield

The barrier is internal. The cost of picking up this bill is not measured in money or in skill, but in a different, psychological currency: the discomfort of exposing yourself, the small toll of embarrassment paid for breaking the pact of silence. That toll is the only thing separating each person from the bill. It is not a pane of glass worth nineteen; it is a few seconds of unease. And those few seconds of unease are, against all proportion, what stop the entire species.

Here is the key to everything, the heart of Part I, and it is worth saying slowly because it is what makes this arbitrage different from any other. In a normal market, an inefficiency closes without everyone having to exploit it; a few are enough. If ten thousand people are too timid, or too slow, or too poor to seize a bargain, it does not matter: as long as a handful of arbitrageurs exist who are none of those things, that handful moves in, shifts the price, and closes the gap for everyone else. The market does not need the crowd to act; it needs a minority immune to what paralyzes the crowd. That minority does the work of correcting the price, and that is why, as soon as the barrier is of a kind that some do not suffer, the arbitrage ends up closing.

What is singular about our case is that the barrier is of a kind that almost no one fails to suffer. Aversion to that toll of embarrassment is not an idiosyncratic trait of the shy; it is a nearly universal property of human wiring, present in different degrees but present in practically everyone. The arbitrageur who ought to come and pick up the bill and close the gap suffers exactly the same toll as everyone else. There is no immune minority waiting to do the work, because the barrier spares almost no one. And a gap that stops everyone equally is closed by no one. The universality of the barrier is not a detail: it is, precisely, the mechanical reason the arbitrage is permanent. It does not close because there is no one safe from what keeps it open.

The scarcity that protects itself

One might object: but some people do bend down. There exist the people who speak in the car, who send the email, who publish. Don't they close the gap, even a little?

No, and for a reason that also illuminates where much of the advantage comes from. They do not close it because they are, and are condemned to remain, few. And here a second mechanism appears that armors the arbitrage: part of its return arises precisely from the fact that almost no one takes it. The person who speaks in the silent car gains a disproportionate advantage in large measure because the other twenty-nine stay quiet; the gesture stands out, is remembered, opens a door, precisely because it is rare. If everyone suddenly spoke, speaking would no longer distinguish anyone, and that portion of the advantage that came from rarity would evaporate. The act returns so much in part because it is scarce.

This means the arbitrage protects itself twice over. It protects itself because the barrier is universal and therefore almost no one comes to close it. And it protects itself because, even if a few do come, their scarcity—guaranteed by that same universal barrier—keeps alive the advantage they collect. Whoever dares does not exhaust the opportunity for others; he merely occupies, almost alone, a very high percentile reached not through extraordinary merit, but through the sheer willingness to pay a toll that almost everyone refuses. It is one of the few ways to stand out enormously without doing anything extraordinary: it is enough to do, sincerely, what almost no one does, knowing that almost no one will do it tomorrow either.

What remains to be explained

With this, Part I has done its work. We have seen that the phenomenon exists: there are acts of negligible cost and open-ended benefit that almost no one performs. We have given it a name: it is an arbitrage, money on the ground, with the astonishing peculiarity that it does not close. And we have located the reason it does not close: the barrier is neither external nor a matter of skill—anyone could bend down—but internal and universal, a small toll of embarrassment that stops almost everyone equally and from which almost no one is safe.

But notice that this answer, though correct, has only moved the mystery inward. We have said the barrier is a toll of embarrassment, a matter of courage. And "courage" and "a small discomfort" are still labels, not explanations. The question grows deeper and more uncomfortable: how can a toll so tiny—a few seconds of discomfort, a risk of rejection that almost never materializes—stop people who are brave in everything else, who face down dangers a thousand times greater without blinking? What is that discomfort made of, what does it contain inside, to outweigh a benefit a hundred times greater than itself?

Answering that requires opening up the toll and looking at its internal accounting, seeing piece by piece how an objectively ridiculous cost manages, at the moment of deciding, to swell until it blots out the sun. That accounting has an exact logic, and it even has a name. It is a tax we levy on ourselves, and it is the subject of the chapter that opens the mechanics of the book.

PART II

The Mechanics

Chapter 4. The Fear Tax

The immediate loss weighs more than the deferred gain.

The previous chapters laid out a puzzle. There is a class of acts whose cost is negligible and whose possible benefit is enormous, anyone can perform them, and yet almost no one does. I said the barrier is not one of skill but of courage, and that this is why the arbitrage does not close. But "courage" names the barrier without explaining it. To name is not to understand. The question is still open, and it is the question of this chapter: if the act is worth so much and costs so little, what exactly is it that stops us? Why does a trivial cost manage, over and over, to halt people who, if they saw the numbers coldly, would cross the street to take that bet?

The answer is that fear levies a tax, and it is worth taking the word seriously, because it is not a loose figure of speech but an exact description of what happens. A tax is a wedge. It drives itself between what an operation returns gross and what the investor keeps net. The operation can be magnificent gross and still not be carried out, if the tax wedge is so wide that net it stops paying. That is what fear does with these acts. The act is worth a great deal gross—that is its objective truth, the one we saw when we measured cost against benefit—but between that true value and the value one feels at the moment of deciding, a wedge inserts itself, and the wedge is so wide that the act reaches consciousness with its sign flipped: something worth a hundred feels like something worth less than nothing.

What makes this tax dangerous is that no state levies it and it appears nowhere. It is invisible, you apply it to yourself, and almost no one ever sees the line on the receipt. And, like the worst taxes, it is not a single rate but an accumulation of distinct levies that all fall on the same transaction and all in the same direction. This chapter is an audit of that accumulation. It is worth breaking it down wedge by wedge, because only when they are seen summed does one understand how a handful of small, measurable distortions manages to invert a bet that ought to be obvious.

The first wedge: a loss weighs more than a gain

The central finding of decision theory over the last half century is simple to state and hard to digest: a loss hurts more than a gain of the same size pleases. Not a little more. Roughly twice as much. The curve that translates what happens to us into what we feel has a steeper slope on the loss side than on the gain side, so that losing a hundred does damage equivalent to gaining two hundred. It is not a defect of a few anxious people; it is the standard shape of the human valuing apparatus, measured again and again, stable across cultures.

Applied to our case, this means the small discomfort of a rejection does not enter the account at its real size, but inflated by a factor. The odd look, the cold reply, the second of ridicule weigh, as they are felt, close to double what they would weigh if the same apparatus measured them without bias. The premium is charged at a markup.

But here we must stop, because this first wedge, by itself, does not explain the puzzle, and pretending it does would be cheating. If a loss weighed twice as much as a gain and the story ended there, we would only decline bets in which the gain is less than twice the loss. And the bets in this book are not like that: in them the possible gain is not twice the cost, it is a hundred times the cost, a thousand times. Doubling the weight of a trivial loss is not enough to overcome a gain a hundred times larger. If loss aversion were all there is, we would take these acts easily, gritting our teeth at a discomfort we know is exaggerated but walking toward the obvious prize. We do not. So there must be something more, something that does not inflate the cost but shrinks the benefit, that grabs that factor of a hundred and reduces it until it fits beneath a minor discomfort. The following wedges do that work.

The second wedge: time flattens the gain

The cost of these acts is paid now. The benefit, when it comes, comes later, and sometimes much later: the acquaintance who opens a door for you does it three years from now, the seeded idea germinates in a decade, the friendship pays out across an entire life. And the human apparatus treats the future in a particular way that in finance has an exact name: it discounts it. It brings future value into the present by applying a rate, and the further off the payout, the more its present value shrinks.

Discounting the future is reasonable; a prize ten years out is worth less today than the same prize in hand. The problem is not that we discount, but the usurious rate at which fear does it. We do not apply a moderate, constant discount; we apply a brutal, disproportionate one to the immediate, which collapses the present value of almost everything that does not happen right now. At that rate, an enormous gain set three years out shrinks to a fraction of itself before reaching consciousness. The prize of a hundred, discounted by fear, enters the account worth ten, or five.

Notice what is happening. The first wedge multiplied the cost by two. The second divided the benefit by ten or twenty. The distance between them, which gross was abysmal in favor of the act, is closing visibly, and we are not done yet.

The third wedge: what is not seen is not recorded

This is the most insidious of all, because it does not shrink the benefit: it erases it from the books.

The cost of these acts is vivid, concrete, observable. You can imagine the rejection in cinematic detail before it happens: the face the other will make, the exact tone of the curt reply, the sensation in your chest. The benefit, by contrast, is invisible by nature, and not by accident, but because it is counterfactual. The friendship you did not begin has no face. The person you would have met if you had spoken does not exist for you; it never came to exist, and so you cannot see it, or miss it, or place it on the scale. We value things by what we manage to picture, and on the benefit side there is nothing to picture: a void with no image.

In accounting terms, the benefit of these acts is an off-balance-sheet asset. It does not appear in the books, and what does not appear in the books is valued at zero—not because it is worth zero, but because the system doing the accounting has nowhere to record it. And so, at the moment of deciding, the scale we weigh does not set a small cost against a large benefit. It sets a small, vivid, present cost against an empty box. And against an empty box, any cost, however tiny, wins. This wedge does not adjust the price of the benefit: it takes it out of the equation entirely. What is compared is not a hundred against two, it is two against nothing.

The fourth wedge: the certain beats the probable

One more asymmetry remains between the two sides. The cost, if the act goes wrong, is nearly certain: if I am rejected, the discomfort arrives, guaranteed. The benefit, by contrast, is probabilistic and of unknown probability: maybe this email, this conversation, this text leads to something, and maybe not, and there is no way to know the true odds.

The human apparatus treats the certain and the probable very differently, and treats the uncertain-uncertain worse still—that whose probabilities cannot even be estimated. We overvalue certainty and distrust what we cannot quantify; we demand of an uncertain gain an exorbitant risk premium before taking it seriously. A small but nearly certain loss feels more real, more worth avoiding, than a large gain of nebulous probability. Again the wedge falls on the same side: it lends solidity to the cost and dissolves the benefit into the fog of what cannot be calculated.

The fifth wedge, the quietest: action is taxed, inaction is not

So far the four wedges explain why the cost inflates and the benefit shrinks. But the quietest and perhaps the most decisive is missing, the one that explains why the starting point is always silence and not speech.

A loss you caused by acting hurts more than an identical loss that arrived from doing nothing. If I say hello and am rejected, the sting is mine, self-inflicted, I caused it, I exposed myself. If I stay quiet and lose the friendship that would have been born, that loss is not only invisible for the reason we saw in the third wedge, but also does not feel like my doing: "nothing happened." The fear apparatus taxes action heavily and gives inaction a free pass. To act pays tax; to abstain does not. And that is why the default state, the position we always start from, is not-doing, because not-doing feels free.

But not-doing is not free. Not-doing is also a choice, with its consequences, as real as any other; the only thing is that it issues no invoice. Silence seems to cost zero only because its cost is of the kind this battery of wedges is designed not to record: deferred, invisible, not attributable to an act of one's own. It is the perfect cost for going unnoticed, and so it goes.

And here is the twist that turns the whole matter inside out. In the moment, we fear the regret of having acted badly: the hot shame of the attempt that came out crooked. But the regret of action is of a kind that cools quickly and is forgotten; no one's old age is ruined by the memory of that greeting that went unreturned. What one knows, looking back over an entire life, is that the regrets that endure, the ones that grow with the years instead of shrinking, are almost always the regrets of inaction: what was not said, what was not sent, the person we did not approach, the work we did not publish. Fear inverts the true calendar of regret. It makes us fear a hot, passing sting in order to push us toward a cold, permanent pain. It taxes savagely exactly the thing—action—that this entire book is about, and exempts exactly the thing—silence—that in the long run is the only thing we will truly regret.

Why social loss is taxed even more

These five wedges tax any loss, of whatever kind. But the loss we are talking about has an aggravating factor: it is social. We are not risking money or an object, we are risking standing, belonging, the other's regard. And the human apparatus treats social rejection not as a nuisance but as something close to a mortal threat: the pain of being snubbed runs through circuits related to those of physical pain. The consequence is a surcharge on all the previous wedges. The loss, already inflated by aversion, attributed to our action, made certain and vivid, receives on top of it a multiplier for the sheer fact of being social, as if that minor rejection staked the expulsion from the tribe and, with it, survival.

Why we are built to treat an odd look as a mortal danger is not a question for this chapter, but for the next, and there I will answer it. For now it is enough to note the surcharge and add it to the account.

The sum, and the deadweight it leaves

Now the wedges can be summed and the full tax seen. Aversion doubles the cost. The usurious discount divides the benefit by ten or twenty. Invisibility takes it straight out of the books. Uncertainty dissolves it into fog. The bias toward inaction makes abstaining seem free. And the social character of the loss multiplies everything. Chained together, these distortions are more than enough to achieve what none would achieve alone: to turn an act worth a hundred gross into an act that, net, at the moment of deciding, feels like a certain loss best avoided. That is the fear tax, and that is the mechanism that was missing beneath the word "courage." It is not that people are cowardly in some vague moral sense. It is that a set of measurable levies, all pushing in the same direction, systematically transforms a good bet into one that feels bad.

And like every high tax, its true cost is not what it collects, but what it prevents. The most expensive thing about a tax is not the discomfort that is paid, but the transactions that never happen because, taxed at that rate, they stop seeming profitable to one of the parties. Economists call it deadweight loss: the value that would have been created and is not, the mutually beneficial exchanges that do not take place. The deadweight loss of the fear tax is incalculable and everywhere. It is the two people who would have been friends forever and pass each other in silence, each convinced the approach was not worth the risk. It is the projects not launched, the emails not sent, the questions not asked, the works finished and shut in a drawer. It is an ocean of connections and creations that never come to exist—not because they were not worth it, but because on both sides of the operation the toll of fear made them look like a bad deal. The inefficiency of chapter three has its invoice here: that is what the unclosed arbitrage leaves on the table, life after life, with no one to pick it up.

With this we have the mechanism. But it is worth seeing precisely what kind of thing we have described, because the next step depends on that precision. Everything in this chapter is, at bottom, a matter of perception. A deformation of the inner scale, a bent lens that makes things look a size they are not. It is, in a word, a bias. And a bias is easy to wave away, because the escape is always there: "that's how it feels to me, and feelings aren't up for debate; I'd rather not do it, and that's my right." As long as this is only a bias, that escape hatch stays open, and with it the declined act can disguise itself as a legitimate preference.

The next chapter closes that hatch. Because what fear deforms is not a vague sense of value that each person is free to feel their own way. It is a precise financial object, with a known shape and a correct valuation that depends on no one's taste. When you see what it is we are really refusing, the error can no longer hide behind the word "preference." It stops being a bias one can claim to own and becomes what it truly is: a mistake in arithmetic.

Chapter 5. Buying Calls on Your Own Life

The profile is convex: bounded loss, open gain.

The previous chapter established that we underinvest in these acts because loss aversion inflates the immediate cost. That is a bias: a distortion of perception, a bent lens. This chapter makes a stronger and more uncomfortable claim. It is not just that we misperceive the cost. It is that these acts have a precise, identifiable financial structure, with a name, and that refusing them is not a matter of taste but an error of valuation. They have the profile of an option. And a cheap option with that profile is not something one can prefer or not prefer, the way one prefers tea to coffee. It is something mispriced. To refuse it is to get the arithmetic wrong, not to exercise a right.

The distinction between a bias and a valuation error matters, and it is worth fixing before we go on. A bias is a tendency: an inclination of judgment one could, in principle, defend as part of one's character. A valuation error is another thing. It is a loss of money that anyone would reverse the instant they saw the true prices. No one defends a valuation error once it is shown to them; they correct it and are embarrassed to have made it. The thesis of this chapter is that whoever does not greet the stranger, does not send the email, does not publish the text, is not exercising a legitimate preference about how to live. They are leaving a bill on the ground because they have miscalculated what it costs to bend down. And the proof that it is an error and not a preference is that, once the calculation is properly explained, almost no one would defend it.

What an option actually is

It is worth being precise, because the whole force of the argument depends on the analogy being exact and not decorative. A call option—a *call*—is the right, but not the obligation, to buy something at a price fixed in advance. Whoever acquires it pays a known amount for that right: the premium. That premium is all they can lose. If the asset does not rise, the option expires worthless and the buyer loses the premium, not a cent more. Their loss is bounded, it has a floor, it is known the day they enter. If the asset rises, by contrast, the gain has no ceiling: the more it rises, the more the right to buy cheap is worth. Loss closed below, gain open above. That asymmetry is the very definition of the instrument.

That asymmetry is called convexity, and it is not a loose word: it describes the shape of the curve relating what you put in to what you take out. In a linear bet, the curve is a straight line: twice the risk, twice the prize, twice the punishment. In a convex position, the curve bends in your favor. The punishment flattens until it touches a floor; the prize steepens without limit. The mathematical consequence of that shape has a name, Jensen's inequality, and it says something that is at first counterintuitive: when the curve is convex, the average result of uncertainty is better than the result of the average. Put without the jargon: a convex position does not merely tolerate uncertainty, it feeds on it. The more dispersed, the wilder, the more unpredictable the possible outcomes, the better it does, because it keeps the good tail and has the bad tail sealed off. Whoever buys an option is not betting on a specific outcome. They are buying dispersion. They are betting that things will happen, without needing to know which.

Keep this, because it is the hinge of the whole book: the convex benefits from what cannot be foreseen. It needs no forecast. It only needs the world to be wide.

The mapping is exact, not approximate

Now the central claim. The acts this book is about—approaching the stranger, asking, publishing, sending the cold email—are call options on your own life, and they are so in the literal sense, not the figurative one. It is worth walking through the mapping piece by piece, because if it fits in every part, the conclusion stops being a pretty metaphor and becomes a fact about the structure of the act.

The premium is the social discomfort. It is a cost known in advance: you know, before you open your mouth, more or less what it feels like to be ignored or looked at oddly. It is bounded: that discomfort has a very low ceiling and a short duration, measured in seconds, not years. And, like every premium, it is paid up front and irreversibly at the moment of taking the position. Here the mapping is finer than it looks. When you say hello, you pay the discomfort on the spot, whether they respond well or badly.

You do not pay it at the end, conditional on the outcome; you pay it on entry, sunk and gone from the first second, exactly like the premium on an option, which leaves your account the day you buy and never returns, however the asset does. The discomfort of greeting is a premium already paid the instant you decide to greet.

The underlying is your life, and its range is wide. What can come out of a conversation begun, an email sent, a text published, runs from absolute nothing—by far the most frequent—to outcomes that change a biography: a thirty-year friendship, a partner, a job, a spouse, an idea that rearranges your head. The distribution of outcomes has a fat, distant right tail. Most attempts return nothing appreciable. A small fraction return disproportionately, and a very few return so much that they justify, on their own, all the other attempts combined.

Bounded premium, paid up front, with no possibility of losing more than that. Open underlying, with a right tail that has no ceiling. That does not resemble a call option: it is a call option. The profile coincides in all its features, not in its atmosphere. And therefore the conclusion is licit: to buy these acts is to buy convexity on the most volatile asset you own, which is what is going to happen to you.

You don't need to win often

Here is the point that separates this argument from cheap cheerleading, from "go for it, you'll see how it all works out." No, it almost never works out. That is precisely the point, and to get it backwards is to lose everything.

A convex position is rational even if it fails the vast majority of the time. It does not need a high hit rate; it needs an asymmetric profile and enough repetitions. If the premium is tiny and the tail is enormous, it is enough for the tail to materialize rarely for the set of bets to have positive value. Venture capital works this way: most of a fund's investments die, and the fund wins because one in ten or one in twenty returns a hundred times what was put in and pays for all the ones that sank. The strategy is not to be right often. It is to be right cheaply and hugely when you are right, and to lose little and known when you are wrong, which is always.

This completely reorders the question. The right question was never "is this stranger going to respond well?" That question assumes, without saying so, that the act is only worth it if it wins, which is the logic of a linear bet, not an option. The right question is: "how much does it cost me to try, and how much can I get the times it works?" If the first is trivial and the second is open, the calculation is done, and the result of an isolated attempt is irrelevant. Whoever evaluates each greeting separately, and gets discouraged because three in a row led nowhere, is making an elementary accounting error: they are judging a portfolio of options by the return on a single one, ignoring that the position is evaluated in aggregate and over time, never position by position. Three options that expire worthless refute nothing. They are the foreseen, budgeted cost of the business.

So the rarity of success, far from being an objection, is part of the design. Whoever does not understand this demands that each attempt pay, and when it does not, quits. Whoever understands it keeps buying cheap premiums calmly, knowing the average does not matter, that the tail matters, and that the tail comes to whoever holds the position open long enough.

Why this is not the lottery

Arriving here, an attentive reader raises a hand with the right objection. A lottery ticket also has that shape: you lose little and known, you can win a fortune. Am I not describing, in elegant vocabulary, an invitation to gamble? The objection is good and the answer is the one that makes the whole argument solid, so it is worth giving slowly.

The convex shape is necessary but not sufficient. A bet can have bounded loss and open gain and still be a bad bet, if the expected value is negative. The lottery is exactly that case. It is designed by a house that keeps a cut, so that the probabilistic sum of all the prizes, minus the cost of the tickets, gives a negative number. The lottery player buys a convex shape with negative expected value: the asymmetry exists, but the tail is so far off and so improbable that, multiplied by its prize, it does not pay for the premium. They buy the illusion of convexity. The curve bends in their favor on the drawing, but the area under the curve, weighted by probability, is in the red.

The acts in this book differ from the lottery on three precise points, and all three pull in the same direction. First: there is no house. No one charges a commission for you to greet a stranger, no one has rigged the game so you lose. There is no bank adjusting the prizes to extract a margin at your expense. That alone already changes the sign of the expected value, because it removes the structural bleed that dooms whoever plays against a house. Second: the tail is infinitely closer. The probability that a cold email, a conversation, a published text leads to something valuable is not one in hundreds of millions; it is, depending on the act, one in five or one in fifty. The frequency of the prize is of a different order of magnitude, and at that frequency convexity does pay. Third, which I will develop in the next chapter on compound interest: the prizes are not independent or terminal like a raffle's. A good outcome opens the door to others. The friendship introduces a third party, the published text draws the reader who becomes a partner. The tail, when it arrives, does not hand over a check and leave; it sows. The lottery pays once and is over. These acts pay and, in paying, multiply the number of future bets.

Three differences, one conclusion: the same convex shape that in the lottery wraps a negative expected value here wraps a positive one. It is not gambling. It is the opposite of gambling. It is taking the side of the table where the house normally sits.

When the act is not convex

A concept that approves of everything is no use for thinking; it only serves to reassure. If convexity were a stamp pressed onto any act of daring, it would be self-help with a mathematical alibi. It is not, and showing where it fails is what gives the argument its edge and its honesty.

Convexity requires that the loss be genuinely bounded. That bound is not a gift; it is a condition to be checked case by case, and there are situations in which it does not hold. If whoever has power over you—your boss, someone your livelihood depends on—is the recipient of the act, the loss stops having a low floor: an unfortunate sentence can cost you much more than thirty seconds of embarrassment, it can cost you your job. There the premium is neither small nor known; it is large and of uncertain tail, and the position is no longer convex, but linear or worse. If the context turns your initiative into an intrusion on someone who cannot leave—because of the place, the asymmetry of power, the situation—the cost you pay is not only yours, and the calculation changes in nature. To that limit, the one separating courage from trespass, I devote an entire chapter later on, because it is the most serious crack in the argument and deserves to be treated without shortcuts.

For now it is enough to fix the rule: the act is convex when, and only when, the loss is genuinely bounded and genuinely yours. Checking that bound before acting is not cowardice; it is the diligence of someone who knows what they are buying. The vast majority of the acts this book is about pass the test with room to spare—talking to a stranger in a line, publishing a text, emailing someone you admire have the most trivial downside there is. But the test exists, and naming it is what distinguishes a thesis from a pep talk.

The error, with its name

Now the error committed by whoever refuses these acts can be stated precisely, and why it is an error and not a preference.

Whoever refuses is mispricing the option, and mispricing it on two sides at once. On one side, they inflate the premium. The loss aversion of the previous chapter makes the social discomfort—which is low, brief, and bounded—feel like an imminent and enormous catastrophe. The body charges the premium as if it were ruinous when it is trivial. On the other side, they ignore the tail. The possible benefit is deferred, invisible in advance, and dispersed, and so it does not enter the account; whoever decides imagines their future as a flat line, with no variance, where "nothing will come of saying hello" is a near-certain prediction. But their future is not a flat line. It is wide, volatile, full of forks that depend precisely on the contacts they initiate. In imagining it flat, they are setting for their own life a volatility close to zero, and at that fictitious volatility the option is worth nothing. On that miscalculation, declining it is coherent. On the true numbers, declining it is giving away the entire tail to avoid paying a premium that does not hurt.

Inflated premium, ignored tail. That is the valuation error, with its two legs. And notice that in neither of them is there a legitimate preference hidden. No one prefers, in cold blood, to overpay for a minor discomfort while renouncing an open-ended gain. That is not a taste; it is a mistake that reverses the moment the real prices are seen, just as no one defends having sold a house for a tenth of its value because they did not know what it was worth.

One last question remains, and with it I close the chapter by handing over the next. In a real market, an option this cheap and this clearly undervalued would not last that way even a minute. Someone would buy it, and then someone else, and another, and in buying it they would drive its price up until the bargain was erased. The arbitrage would close, as all of them close. Why does this one not close? Why does the option stay lying on the ground, undervalued, decade after decade, without the crowd of arbitrageurs pouncing on it?

The answer is that the error is not some people's. It is nearly everyone's, and it is the same in everyone. No arbitrageur arrives to correct the price because the arbitrageur suffers exactly the same aversion as the rest: he too inflates the premium and he too ignores the tail. The hand that ought to pick up the bill trembles for the same reason as all the others. And an error shared by the entire species is not arbitraged: it is perpetuated. This forces us to the question of the next chapter, which is no longer financial but older. If declining these options is an error so clear, so cheap to correct, so universal, then it cannot be an accident of calculation. It has to be written into us. We have to be built to commit it. And we are: the fear that inflates the premium was not born in a market, it was born in a tribe, and to that tribe we still carry inside is dedicated what follows.

Chapter 6. The Tribe We Carry Inside

Fear is an ancient adaptation, miscalibrated today. It is not stupidity.

So far the book has proven something and left it unexplained. It has proven that the fear of these acts is disproportionate: it inflates a trivial cost until it blots out everything, and it does so in a way so systematic, so universal, so repeated across people of every culture and every temperament, that it can no longer be treated as an individual defect or as simple shyness. A distortion that appears in nearly every human being, with the same shape, generation after generation, is not an accident or a failing of the shy. It is a trait of the species. It is built into us. And what is built into a species was, by definition, built for some reason. The question of this chapter is what that reason was: why evolution equipped us with a mechanism that so reliably makes us refuse good bets.

The most useful answer I know comes from thinking of fear not as an emotion but as a risk model: a system that estimates the danger of a situation and charges, in the form of anticipated discomfort, a premium proportional to that danger. Every risk model is calibrated with data, with the accumulated experience of which situations proved lethal and which harmless. And here is the key to the whole chapter: the risk model we carry inside was calibrated with data from a world that no longer exists. It still runs, still charges premiums, still issues alarms, but it computes them according to the conditions of an environment that vanished millennia ago. It is an inherited system, still running in production, with parameters no one has readjusted since the world changed completely.

When a look really was a matter of life and death

For almost the whole history of our species, human beings lived in small tribes, of a few dozen or at most around a hundred and fifty individuals, that you could not leave. There was no other tribe around the corner, no anonymous city to move to, no way to rebuild a life among strangers. The group you were born into was the only world available, and your survival depended entirely on your place in it.

Food was shared according to status. Protection from predators and from other groups depended on having allies. Your chances of reproducing depended on your reputation within the group. In that world, social position was not a luxury or a vanity: it was, literally and directly, the substrate of life.

And therefore social disapproval was not a nuisance. It was a first-order danger signal. Being disliked, humiliated, losing prestige before the group, becoming an object of mockery or rejection—all of that threatened the one thing keeping you alive, which was your bond with the group. At the extreme, rejection took the form of ostracism, expulsion, and expulsion from the group was equivalent to a death sentence: alone, without allies, without shared food, a human being in the wild did not last. So the risk model did, in that environment, exactly what it should. When it estimated that an act might cost you status and charged a very high premium of fear for it, it was not wrong. It charged dearly because the danger was dear. The premium was well calculated, tuned to a world where a look of contempt could be, at the end of a chain of consequences, a matter of life and death.

When today you feel that tightening in the chest before speaking to a stranger, you are not feeling an absurd reaction. You are feeling the output of a risk model that was, in its day, rigorously correct.

Why the model prefers to err on the side of fear

There is one more feature of the inherited system worth understanding, because it explains not just that the fear exists, but that it is so exaggerated. Risk models forged by evolution do not seek the most accurate estimate possible; they seek the one that minimizes the cost of being wrong. And being wrong has two forms, with very different costs.

You can err by omission: treating as harmless something that was dangerous. In the ancestral world, that kind of error was paid dearly, sometimes with your life: whoever did not fear the group's contempt enough, and acted in a way that isolated him, died. And you can err by excess: treating as dangerous something that was harmless. That kind of error cost only a little useless discomfort, a few calories of stress spent for nothing. Between an error that kills you and an error that makes you uncomfortable, evolution always chooses the second. It calibrates the alarm to go off too much, not too little, because a thousand false alarms cost less than a single undetected fire.

It is the logic of the smoke detector, which shrieks at the burnt toast not because it is stupid, but because the designer preferred a thousand annoyances to a house on fire. Our social fear works the same way. It is deliberately biased toward the false alarm, tuned to overestimate the danger of exposure, because in the environment where that bias was calibrated it saved lives. The disproportion we denounced in the previous chapters—a cost of seconds felt as a catastrophe—is not, then, a failure of the system. It is the system doing exactly what it was designed to do: err on the side of caution, just in case.

The regime changed; the model did not

Everything above explains that the fear was correct. It does not yet explain why it harms us today. The answer is that between the world for which the model was calibrated and the world in which we use it there is a total discontinuity, a change of regime so complete that it entirely inverts the data the system was trained on.

We no longer live in tribes we cannot leave. We live among millions of strangers, in an environment defined by anonymity and by the permanent possibility of leaving. The stranger in the car you are afraid to speak to is not a member of your tribe whose judgment will determine your access to food for the next thirty years. He is someone you will never see again, whose opinion of you will not have the slightest consequence on your material life five minutes from now, when each of you gets off at your stop. A rejection from him costs you no protection, no food, no allies, no reputation before anyone who matters, because he is not part of any group you depend on. In the ancestral world, the chain linking another's contempt to real danger was short and firm. In today's world, that chain is cut: a stranger's contempt no longer leads anywhere.

The data changed completely, but the model was not recalibrated. It still estimates social risk as if we lived in the tribe, still treats every interaction with a stranger as if that stranger's judgment could ruin us, still charges the very high premium that corresponded to a danger that no longer exists. It is a risk model trained on data from a vanished regime and applied, without adjustment, to a new regime where that data no longer holds. In finance, a model like that—one that keeps pricing risk according to conditions that no longer apply—produces guaranteed and often ruinous errors, and no competent manager would leave it running. We leave it running, because we do not choose our risk models: we inherit them, and evolution recalibrates on a timescale of millennia, not generations. The world transformed in a few thousand years, a blink in evolutionary terms, and our fear system still has not gotten the news that the tribe is gone.

What this diagnosis allows, and what it does not

Seeing fear this way has two consequences that matter for everything that follows, and they are worth separating because they pull in opposite directions.

The first is that it disarms contempt. Whoever does not dare is neither a coward nor a fool; he is someone obeying a risk model that was correct for two million years and that is still, understandably, switched on. The aversion we feel is not a weakness of character, it is an inheritance, the same in the bold executive as in the shy teenager, because neither of them chose his wiring. This also closes the last remaining link on why the arbitrage does not close: the barrier is universal because it is of the species, not of the individual. We all run the same inherited model, we all pay the same inflated premium, and that is why there is no immune person who comes to pick up the bill from the ground. And it also explains that surcharge I noted without justifying: why social loss weighs more than any other. It weighs more because, of all the categories of danger, the social was the one most directly tied to survival, and therefore the one that received the most sensitive and loudest alarm.

The second consequence pulls against the first, and it must be said with the same clarity. That the fear has an honorable origin does not make it reliable. To understand that a risk model is miscalibrated is not a reason to respect its estimates; it is the exact reason to stop trusting them. An inherited system that prices according to a world that no longer exists does not deserve obedience for being venerable; it deserves to be worked around. And here is the delicate point: fear cannot be recalibrated from within. You can speak to a thousand strangers and verify a thousand times that nothing happened, and the alarm will keep sounding the thousand-and-first time with the same force, because it does not learn at the pace of your experience but at the pace of the evolution of the species.

You are not going to convince your fear. The correction cannot come from feeling differently; it has to come from deciding differently, from placing an explicit calculation ahead of a premium you know is false, from treating the alarm as the beep of an old detector that goes off at the toast and that you no longer heed even as it keeps sounding.

With this, the mechanics of fear are complete. We know it inflates the cost, we know why it inflates it, and we know its verdict is not to be trusted no matter how ancient it is. But everything said so far has dealt with only one side of the scale: the cost, and its exaggeration. The other side is missing. Because the inherited model not only overcharges the premium; it is also blind to something essential about the gain, something that did not exist in its original world and that in ours changes everything. It was calibrated in an environment where each interaction was an isolated event, with an outcome that began and ended there. It has no way to represent that, in a connected world like ours, these acts do not add: they multiply. And that blindness to multiplication—to the way a single small act can compound over an entire life—is what makes us underestimate the benefit as much as we overestimate the cost. To that other half of the error, the one on the gain side, the next chapter is dedicated.

Chapter 7. The Compound Interest of Small Acts

The effects multiply, they do not add.

All the mechanics we have seen dealt with one side of the scale. We proved that the cost of these acts is small, that fear inflates it, and why it inflates it: an inherited risk model, calibrated for a world that no longer exists, that errs on the side of caution by design. But a scale has two pans, and until now we have not looked at the second. What is missing is to understand the gain: not whether it is high—we took that as observed in Part I—but what shape it has, how it behaves, why it escapes us even when we try to measure it honestly.

And here a second error of the inherited model appears, distinct from inflating the cost and, if anything, deeper. The model not only overcharges for risk; it is also structurally incapable of seeing how the benefit grows. It was calibrated in the tribe, where your social world was a closed set of a few dozen people you already knew. In that world there was no network to expand: you could not add nodes, the graph was closed, and each interaction was an isolated event with a consequence bounded within a fixed set of ties. Compounding a social network over time was, there, literally impossible, and that is why the model never needed to represent that possibility and does not represent it. The same change of regime that cut the cost—the stranger you will never see again—opened the benefit: in a world of millions of nodes and unlimited ties, those acts that in the tribe were one-time events become investments that compound. The tribe that vanished freed us twice over: it lowered what we risk and uncovered what we can gain. This chapter is about that second half.

The thesis is simple to state and hard to feel in its full magnitude: these acts do not add, they multiply. And multiplication sustained over time is the most powerful and least understood force operating on a human life.

Adding and multiplying are not relatives

It is worth pausing on the difference between adding and multiplying, because almost the whole valuation error of the benefit is born from underrating it. Linear growth adds a constant amount each period: you take a step, another step, another step, and advance predictably and modestly. Compound growth multiplies by a factor each period, and does something the human intuition does not process well: for a long time it resembles the linear, is almost indistinguishable from it, and then, all at once, it shoots up with a violence no linear accumulation can ever reach.

The arithmetic is merciless and worth seeing bare. A daily edge of one percent, compounded over a year, does not leave you three or four percent better: it multiplies you by nearly thirty-eight. One point zero one raised to three hundred and sixty-five gives around thirty-seven and a half times. The same figure with no edge, one raised to any power, stays at one. A one percent per day, an imperceptible difference from one day to the next, invisible in any snapshot, separates after a year a life multiplied by thirty-eight from a life that did not move. And conversely: a daily erosion of one percent, zero point nine-nine raised to three hundred and sixty-five, does not leave you at ninety-something percent, it leaves you at two and a half. Almost everything lost, a grain each day.

The human mind thinks by default in straight lines, and that is why compound growth always ambushes it. It is the old parable of the pond whose lily pad doubles its surface every day: if it takes forty-eight days to cover the whole pond, on what day is it half covered? Day forty-seven. Until the second-to-last day, the pond seems almost empty, and the linear observer swears there is a long way to go. Here is the key to why we underestimate the benefit of these acts even when we stop ignoring it: it is not only invisible in advance, as we saw; it is that, even when we try to estimate it, we add where we should multiply, and so we always calculate it low, always by an enormous factor.

Why these acts multiply, and it is not a figure of speech

One should be suspicious if this were only an inspiring metaphor. It is not; the mechanism of multiplication is concrete and can be named. What makes something compound, in any domain, is that its returns are reinvested in the base they come from. Interest compounds because this year's interest is added to the principal and generates interest next year. The right question, then, is whether the return on these acts is reinvested in the base. And it is reinvested, by two well-documented routes.

The first is the network. A new tie hands you not just that person; it hands you access to the people that person knows, and to the people those know. Each node you add does not grow in isolation: it connects with the rest and multiplies the possible connections of the whole set. The network grows faster than the number of people in it, because what matters is not the nodes but the links, and the links explode as the network fills. Each conversation begun that catches does not add a contact: it reinvests in a fabric that from then on generates contacts on its own.

The second is cumulative advantage, what sociologists call the Matthew effect, after the saying that to whoever has, more will be given. A published work attracts opportunities more or less in proportion to what you have already done and to how visible you are; each text, each finished project, thickens a body of work that from a certain point begins to attract on its own, without your having to push each time from zero. Reputation works the same way: each act that goes well makes the next one land better, gets the door opened faster, gets you the benefit of the doubt. The capital on which you compound is not money, it is your network, your body of work, and your reputation, and each act that catches reinvests in that capital and raises the base on which everything you do afterward will grow.

One should be honest, as we were when speaking of arbitrage: this compounds more noisily and less reliably than a bank account. The rate is variable, the process is random, there are drops and flat stretches, and no one guarantees you thirty-eight to one. But the structure is multiplicative, and on average, sustained over time, the structure prevails over the noise. It is not necessary that every act reinvest; it is enough for the reinvestment to happen often enough for the curve to pull away from the line. And it pulls away.

The exponent is time

There is a feature of compound interest that changes everything once it is understood, and it is where time lives in the formula. In linear growth, time is one more factor, one that adds. In compound growth, time is in the exponent, and what occupies the exponent dominates everything else. That is why, in compounding, starting early beats starting big. A few years' head start, placed in the exponent, weigh more than an enormous difference in the initial amount, because the exponent does not add years of benefit: it multiplies them.

This completely reorders the value of acting today. Whoever begins at twenty to speak, to ask, to publish, to approach, and whoever begins at forty with twice the talent and twice the resources, do not end up with a difference of twenty years of linear benefit. They end up with the difference between two exponents, and that difference is of another nature, categorical, impossible to recover no matter how hard the second tries later. Compound interest is, at bottom, an arbitrage on time: it converts early patience into an advantage no late intensity can match. And it is an arbitrage almost no one seizes, not for lack of means, but out of impatience and, above all, out of not seeing the curve: at the start, when the line and the exponential almost touch, acting today seems to return so little that one postpones it, without knowing that one is giving away precisely the exponent years that are worth the most.

Why the gap widens

This resolves a puzzle noted in Part I and left unexplained: why the distance between those who do these acts and those who do not grows over time instead of holding steady. If the benefit were linear, whoever dares would run a bit ahead, a constant and modest advantage. But the benefit is not linear, and two people who differ by a small rate per period do not separate by a fixed distance: they diverge exponentially. Whoever dares is not a bit ahead; he is on another curve. And the distance between two exponential curves does not widen little by little, it explodes.

Hence, seen from outside, the life of someone who has practiced these acts for decades seems to require extraordinary luck or uncommon talent, when it required neither. It required a small, slightly positive rate, sustained for a long time. It is the conclusion that synthesizes all the mechanics of the book: these acts are, each of them, convex bets—bounded loss, open gain, as we saw—whose winning tail, when it comes, does not pay once and leave, but is reinvested and compounds. Convexity and compounding together are the whole engine. The first guarantees that you risk little and can gain much on each attempt; the second guarantees that what you gain multiplies over a life. A handful of cheap bets whose rare prizes compound: that is what separates, after thirty years, two biographies that began identical.

The other edge of the curve

Compounding has an edge that cuts in the opposite direction, and to omit it would be to keep the optimistic half of a truth that is not optimistic, but simply exact. Not doing these acts does not leave you still. In a world where others compound, standing still is falling behind, and falling behind is also exponential. The widening gap widens on both sides: not only because whoever acts shoots up, but because whoever does not act sinks relative to him at the same relentless speed.

And there is something worse than standing still, because part of the base erodes on its own if it is not reinvested. The friendship you do not cultivate cools, the skill you do not exercise atrophies, the reputation of someone who never shows up compounds in the negative, grain by grain, like the zero point nine-nine. So the fear tax, which in chapter four seemed a toll paid once for each act not performed, is in reality far more expensive than it appeared. It is not a one-off toll: it is a drag on the growth rate of an entire life. And a drag on the rate is the most expensive thing there is, because it does not subtract an amount, it subtracts an exponent, and compounds against you every day for the rest of your years. A few tenths scraped off your life rate are worth, over a lifetime, more than almost any sum you could lose all at once.

Closing the mechanics

With this, the machine is fully in view, and Part I receives its complete explanation. Recall the puzzle from the beginning: a good deal, cheap and accessible, that almost no one takes and that never runs out. Now we know exactly why. The cost is small and overvalued by an inherited risk model that errs on the side of caution by design and that was calibrated for a vanished world. And the benefit is large and undervalued not once, but three times over: it is invisible in advance, so it does not enter the account; it has a convex shape, so rejecting it for its most probable outcome is a valuation error; and it compounds over time, so even when we estimate it, we estimate it by adding what we should multiply. A bet with the wrong sign in each of its terms: overpriced in the cost, triple-underpriced in the gain. It is no wonder almost no one takes it. The wonder would be to take it, and that is why whoever takes it gains so much.

With the machine understood, the question changes in nature. Until now we asked why: why the phenomenon exists, why it persists, why we resist it. From here on the question is which: which, concretely, are the acts that have this structure, and how they differ according to where they point. Because an act directed at another person, one directed at the work one does, and one directed at oneself are not the same; each direction hides its own trap and its own reward. The catalog that follows walks through them in that order, and begins with the most elementary of all, the one that opened this book in the car: approaching a stranger.

PART III

The Catalog

Chapter 8. Speaking to Strangers

Toward others: we mispredict how the other will react.

With this chapter the book's task changes. The first two parts explained why the phenomenon exists and why it persists; they built the machine and left it in view. What comes now is the catalog: the concrete acts that have this structure, walked through according to where they point. It is worth saying from the start how these chapters work, because they are not what a reader might expect. I do not prove again in each act that the bet is convex and that it compounds; that was established in the mechanics and holds for all of them equally. What each catalog chapter does is something else: it shows that a family of acts really does have that structure, and adds the argument specific to that direction, the trap and the reward particular to it and not shared with the others. The advice, when it appears, is the consequence, never the content.

Let us begin with the most elementary, the one that opened the book in the car: addressing another person. Under this direction—toward others—fall the act of speaking to a stranger, of asking, of thanking and praising, and of keeping your word. And they all share an argument of their own, distinct from the general mechanics, which is the heart of this chapter: beyond fear inflating the cost, something more concrete and more measurable happens. We systematically mispredict how the other will react. It is not only that we fear paying the toll; it is that we are wrong, always in the same direction, about what lies on the other side. And this time it need not be taken on argument: it is measured.

The error has the shape of a biased estimate

It is worth specifying what kind of error this is, because it is not the one we already treated. In the mechanics we saw that the gain of these acts is uncertain, and that this uncertainty, far from being a problem, was favorable because of convexity: bounded loss, open tail. That was a matter of variance, of the dispersion of outcomes. What this chapter is about is different. It is not that the result is uncertain; it is that our central estimate of that result—our forecast of the midpoint, of the most likely—is skewed. And skewed always to the same side: the pessimistic one.

In the language of someone who models risk, the difference is the one between a noisy estimator and a biased estimator. A noisy estimator errs sometimes high and sometimes low, and on average is right; it is corrected by repeating and averaging. A biased estimator errs always in the same direction, and that is why it is much worse: no matter how many times you use it, the bias does not wash out, it survives all experience. Our forecast about how the other will react is a biased estimator. Every time we imagine approaching a stranger, asking a favor, or paying a compliment, we overestimate the friction—the rejection, the discomfort, the annoyance we will cause—and underestimate the warmth—the pleasure, the willingness to help, the delight of being noticed. It is not that we are sometimes too optimistic and sometimes too pessimistic. It is that we err toward the same side, every time, in every act of this family. We are, put in the language of the book, mispricing the counterparty, and not for lack of information about a particular case, but out of a stable prejudice about the counterparty in general.

Speaking

The cleanest case is the one that gives the chapter its name. A now-famous experiment asked commuter-train passengers to do one of two things on their ride: some were to strike up a conversation with the stranger next to them, others were to stay quiet and enjoy their solitude. Before boarding, almost all predicted the same thing: that talking would be the worst, that the other would not want to be bothered, that the silent trip would be more pleasant. The result was the opposite on every front. Those who spoke reported a more pleasant ride than those who stayed quiet. The strangers who were approached not only were not bothered, but also enjoyed it. And the prediction that the other would prefer to be left alone turned out to be wrong at the root.

To that error is added another, measured again and again, which has been called the liking gap: after a conversation, we systematically underestimate how much the other liked us and how much they enjoyed the encounter. We leave convinced we made a worse impression than we made, and the gap persists even among people who end up becoming friends. So in the act of speaking to a stranger two skewed estimates accumulate: we believe the other will not want to talk, and we believe, once we have talked, that we came across worse than we did. Both false, both in the direction that stops us.

Asking

Asking concentrates the bias in an even costlier way, because what we underestimate is not just a diffuse pleasantness, but something with direct consequences: how many people will say yes. The studies on this are remarkably consistent. When a real favor is asked of strangers, the proportion who agree is far higher than the asker anticipates; the asker calculates they will have to approach nearly twice as many people as they actually need to get the same number of yeses. We live convinced we will be rejected far more than we are.

And there is another layer. We overestimate the burden we impose, and underestimate that helping usually feels good to the helper, and that being chosen for a favor often flatters rather than annoys. Here a fine trap appears that is worth naming, because it disguises itself as virtue: we tend not to ask so as not to inconvenience the other, and we tell ourselves it is out of consideration. But consideration is, frequently, an alibi. What we are really avoiding is not the other's discomfort, which we have exaggerated, but our own: the small unease of exposing ourselves to a no. Caring for the other is the story we tell fear so it looks like generosity. Most of the time, in not asking, we protect no one; we merely fail to collect a help that was available.

Thanking and praising

The same bias governs the acts that ask for nothing, but give: thanks and praise. It has been studied what happens when someone writes a sincere letter of gratitude to another person. The writer tends to postpone it and downplay it, because they anticipate it will be somewhat awkward, a little clumsy, that the recipient will not quite know how to receive it. And they are wrong on both counts: they underestimate how much it moves and surprises the one who receives it, and overestimate the discomfort, which barely appears. With compliments it is the same. We keep sincere praise to ourselves—for a stranger over something they are wearing, for a colleague over something they did—because we foresee an awkwardness that does not arrive, and we undervalue the warmth that praise would have left.

Notice that here the unspoken praise or thanks is a perfect case of that deadweight loss I spoke of when treating the fear tax. Both parties would have gained: the giver, from the pleasure of giving it; the receiver, from the pleasure of receiving it. Neither loses anything. And yet the transaction does not happen, not because it is not worth it, but because a skewed estimate of the other's reaction makes it seem riskier than it is. It is value that existed, that was within reach of a two-second gesture, and that evaporates without anyone enjoying it.

Why the error always points the same way

Let us pause on the most important thing, which is not any of these findings separately but their pattern. Speaking, asking, thanking, praising are very different acts from one another. And yet the error we make with all of them is the same and points in the same direction: overestimate the friction, underestimate the warmth. An error this consistent across situations this diverse is not noise. It is the signature of a biased estimator, of a background prejudice about others that we drag into every encounter. And like every bias, it is not corrected by experience: you can verify a hundred times that the stranger responded well, that the favor was granted, that the compliment pleased, and on the hundred-and-first your forecast will again be pessimistic, with the same stubbornness with which the alarm of chapter six sounds again no matter how many times it is shown to be false.

It is no coincidence that it is the same stubbornness, because it is the same mechanism. The biased estimator this chapter measures and the miscalibrated risk model that chapter six explained are one thing seen from two angles. The inherited model was calibrated for a world where the stranger could be a rival, where asking could betray weakness before whoever decided your fate, where exposing yourself to the group was dangerous. In that world, a pessimistic forecast about another's reaction was prudent. The laboratory experiments I have just cited are not discovering a new defect; they are measuring, with stopwatch and questionnaire, exactly the distance between what that old model predicts and what today's world delivers. The liking gap, the underestimation of help, the awkwardness that does not arrive: all of that is the size of the model's error, quantified. And that size is, in each case, the gain we leave on the table.

The one apart: keeping your word

One act in this family remains that runs on another logic, and it is worth being honest and not forcing it into the mold. Keeping your word—doing what you said you would do, showing up when you said you would show up—also points toward others, but its value does not come from mispredicting the other's reaction. It comes from scarcity. And here the bias, curiously, works in our favor if we understand it.

We tend to assume others are as reliable as we mean to be, and so we believe that keeping one's word is normal, expected, something that distinguishes no one. It is a skewed estimate, but this time about the baseline of the population, not about a particular person: we overestimate how many people keep their word. The reality is that pure reliability is rare, so rare that merely having it is enough to stand out. Because most people have learned, from experience, to expect little—promises that dissolve, deadlines that slip, words that are not kept—whoever simply keeps their word lands in a very high percentile without doing anything extraordinary, just by occupying a space almost everyone leaves empty. It is the same percentile logic we saw in Part I, applied here: you do not win by shining, you win because the bar is on the floor and it is enough for you not to let it drop. In the other acts of this chapter, the world's bias about others' reactions harms us and must be overcome. In this one, the world's bias about general reliability benefits us, and one need only take advantage of it by keeping one's word.

Where we go next

All the acts of this chapter share that there is, across from us, another person we model badly. The error lives in the counterparty: in what we believe the stranger feels, the favored one bears, the praised one suffers, the rest of people do. Correcting the act runs, in every case, through correcting the portrait we make of the other.

But there are equally valuable acts in which there is no counterparty to misread, or in which the counterparty is an anonymous public, or the work itself, or no one. There the friction is no longer the fear of someone's reaction, but something different: the difficulty of finishing what was begun and the vertigo of exposing it. Publishing what you made, completing what almost everyone abandons half-done, do not depend on guessing another person right, but on overcoming a scarcity that is somewhere else. To that second direction of the catalog, the one pointing toward the work, the next chapter is dedicated.

Chapter 9. Publish and Finish

Toward the work: the scarcity is in finishing and exposing, not in starting.

Toward others, the error lived in the counterparty: in the wrong portrait we made of another person. Toward the work, there is no counterparty to misread, or there is one only in a diffuse and anonymous form. Here the friction is of another kind, and to locate it we can lean on an elementary economic principle that runs through this whole chapter: return always concentrates in what is scarce. The abundant charges no premium, however good it is; the scarce takes the rent. So the right question, when it comes to the work one does, is not which part is hardest or which looks best, but which is genuinely scarce. In the chain running from the idea to the finished and exposed work, where is the bottleneck? Because there, and only there, is the money.

The answer is the thesis of this chapter, and it contradicts almost everyone's instinct. The scarcity is not in having ideas, nor in starting. It is in finishing, in exposing, and beneath both, in the one raw material both require: sustained attention. Those are the scarce links, and that is why they are the ones that pay.

Starting is abundant, and the abundant is worthless

Let us begin with what is in surplus. Ideas are dirt cheap and everywhere; almost anyone has several good ones a week and does nothing with them. Starting is just as abundant: we all launch projects, draft first pages, sketch plans, open documents we will never touch again. The world is full of beginnings. And the beginning is, besides, addictive, because it delivers the pleasant part without charging the hard one: the novelty, the illusion of the imagined work in its perfect version, the rush of possibility. Starting feels productive and is not, for the same reason it is worthless: because it is abundant and nearly free.

A market does not pay for what is in surplus. No one gives you anything for having had the idea that a thousand others also had, nor for having started what almost everyone starts. The graveyard of half-done things is immense, and it is full precisely because entering it costs nothing. The abundance of beginnings is so great that their market value is, precisely, zero. And yet most people invest there almost all their creative effort: in starting, in starting again, in having one more idea. It is like hoarding the most common raw material in the world and expecting someone to pay a premium for it.

Finishing is the bottleneck

Where almost everyone abandons is in the stretch running from the beginning to the end, and that is why that stretch is the scarce one. Finishing requires crossing the part that has no immediate reward: the middle without novelty, where the work stops being fun and becomes labor; the point where the distance between the imagined work and the real work becomes visible and hurts; the end, where there is no longer any illusion pushing and only the craft of closing remains. There the vast majority falls. Not for lack of talent or ideas, but because finishing is boring, is hard, and gives no dopamine, and the next beginning, with all its promise intact, always turns out more tempting than the laborious closing of the previous one.

Precisely because almost everyone falls there, finishing is the constraint that governs the whole system. In any production process, what fixes the output is not the abundance of the easy stages, but the capacity of the bottleneck; improving anything else is useless if the bottleneck does not widen. The real productivity of a creative life is not fixed by the rate at which you have ideas, which is high in almost everyone, but by the rate at which you finish them, which in almost everyone is close to zero. And since the rent concentrates in the scarce, whoever simply finishes things collects a disproportionate return, not because their works are better than others', but because they exist and others' stayed in the drawer of beginnings. The world is packed with people who had your same idea; it is nearly empty of people who finished it.

There is, besides, a reason that connects to the mechanics: only the finished can compound. We saw that the benefit of these acts multiplies because the returns are reinvested in your base, in your body of work, in your reputation. But a half-done work reinvests nothing; it does not thicken the body, does not attract opportunity, does not exist as far as compound interest is concerned. Finishing is not just crossing a line: it is the condition for the work to enter the machine that compounds. Every thing left half-done is a return that never begins to capitalize.

Exposing is almost pure courage

And yet finishing is not enough, because the finished work kept in the drawer does not pay either. The act of exposing it is missing, and it is here that this chapter touches the heart of the book head-on. Finishing is scarce above all for reasons of effort: it tires, it bores, it costs. Exposing is scarce for a purer and more personal reason: the fear of judgment. The finished work in the drawer costs nothing while it stays hidden, and costs everything the instant you show it. Publishing is the act in which the toll is almost entirely the toll of courage, naked exposure, without the alibi of effort that at least justified the delay in the case of finishing.

Notice that publishing is the cleanest possible example of buying a convex option, exactly as we described it. The cost is bounded: in the worst case, indifference, or some criticism that stings a few days and is forgotten. The gain is open: the reader who becomes a collaborator, the work that finds its people, the reputation that begins to compound, any of the tails the mechanics already taught us to value. Loss closed, gain open, premium tiny. The finished and unpublished work is the purest form of the twenty on the ground: the work is already done, the sunk cost is already paid, and only a gesture with almost no risk is missing to collect what it might return. And almost no one makes that gesture.

It is worth noting a difference from the previous chapter, because it opens the door to the next. When you publish, there is indeed a feared judgment, but it is not that of a specific counterparty you are misreading in real time, like the stranger in the car. It is the verdict of an anonymous, silent, mostly imaginary crowd. Almost no one will say anything to you; the public that truly paralyzes you is not out there responding, it is inside your head, rehearsed in advance. And that means the fear of exposing is no longer entirely an error about another, as in chapter eight; it begins to be an error about a judge we carry with us. It is the first step of a movement inward that the catalog will complete in its last direction.

Beneath it all, attention

Finishing and exposing rest on a single raw material, and it is the scarcest of all: the capacity to sustain attention. Nothing gets finished without staying with it through the boring stretch; you cannot expose what you have not managed to finish. Both scarce links depend on a resource that today is becoming scarce at an unprecedented speed, because we live, for the first time in history, inside an economy explicitly designed to take it from us.

Half a century ago, an economist observed that when information becomes abundant, what becomes scarce is attention, because information consumes attention and suddenly there is a great deal of information competing for very little. That observation, true then, today describes an entire industry. A large part of the current economy is devoted, with enormous resources and talent, to bidding for your attention and taking it. In that environment, keeping the governance of your own attention stops being a productivity trick and becomes something else: possession of the one input everything else depends on, at the very moment the world is trying as never before to take it from you. And there is the largest arbitrage available today, for a purely economic reason: the scarcer a resource is and the more everyone else loses it, the greater the return on keeping it. Deep attention is not valuable despite the economy of distraction; it is valuable precisely because of it, and its value rises every day distraction advances. Whoever keeps their attention intact while everyone around them has theirs fragmented is not resisting an annoying fad: they are sitting on the asset whose price rises fastest, and they have it for free.

And it compounds, like everything in this book. Sustained attention builds skill and a body of work, which in turn compound; fragmented attention builds nothing, it dissipates without leaving sediment. Two people with the same talent, one capable of an hour of focus and the other chopped into minutes, do not separate little by little: they diverge, again, exponentially.

The scarce link

Recapping the logic of the chapter: the return on work concentrates in its scarce links, and the scarce links are finishing, exposing, and the attention both require. Having ideas and starting are crowded oceans where no one collects a premium because supply is in surplus. Finishing, publishing, and sustaining attention are, by contrast, nearly empty terrain, available to anyone and occupied by very few, and that is why they pay so much. It is, once again, the structure of the whole arbitrage of the book: cheap to do, because no one stops you from finishing what you started, publishing what you finished, or protecting your own attention; high-return, because there is the bottleneck where the rent concentrates; and uncollected, because the barrier is internal, made of the tedium of finishing, the fear of exposing, and the discomfort of resisting distraction.

Notice, to close, where the friction has been shifting across the catalog. Toward others, the obstacle was another person: the stranger we read wrong. Toward the work, the obstacle was, in part, a public, but a public we already noticed is more imaginary than real, more an inner judge than a full room. In the act of exposing, something began to show that the last direction of the catalog carries all the way: that sometimes there is no other across from us, not even an anonymous one, and the only one who judges, the only one who prevents the act, is ourselves. The acts directed toward oneself—refusing, admitting you do not know, changing your mind, being alone—have no counterparty at all. The judge is no longer outside. It has moved inside. And to that internalized judge, the hardest of all because it cannot be left behind at any station, the next chapter is dedicated.

Chapter 10. Saying No

Toward oneself: here the judge is already internalized.

In the two previous directions of the catalog there was, across from us, someone. Toward others, a stranger, a favored one, a praised one, whom we read wrong. Toward the work, a public, though we already noticed it was more imaginary than real, more inner judge than full room. In this last direction there is no one. The acts directed toward oneself—refusing, setting a limit, admitting you do not know, changing your mind, being alone—have no counterparty at all to misread. And yet the friction not only remains, but is often the most tenacious of all. That is the puzzle particular to this chapter, and its answer is the one that orders everything that follows: if there is no one across from us and something still stops us, then the judge we fear is not across from us. It is inside. We have swallowed it, and now we perform for a spectator who lives in our own head.

In the financial language of the book, this describes the strangest situation of all: we are paying a real premium—the same old toll of fear—to a counterparty that does not exist. A judge with no body, no reaction, no positions on the other side of the operation. And there is a consequence that makes this the hardest direction of the catalog. In all the previous cases, however skewed our forecast, there remained a thread tying it to an external reality capable, in principle, of correcting it: the real stranger was kind, the real crowd was indifferent, the real work did compound, and it was enough to look for the price to readjust. Here that thread is cut. The judge is imaginary and the accounting it keeps is too, so no outside reality can ever force a revaluation. It is the most armored prediction error there is, a closed loop that feeds on itself, because it has internalized both the asset and the market. There is no external market maker who comes to set the fair price, because the entire market is inside a single head.

Where the judge comes from

It is worth understanding where that inner spectator comes from, because it is not a personal defect or a quirk, but one more piece of the same ancient machinery we have been dismantling. The inherited risk model of chapter six did not merely give us fear of real disapproval. It gave us something more sophisticated and more useful for surviving in the tribe: a simulator of the group's judgment, capable of anticipating how others would react before they reacted, so as to correct course in time. To rehearse inwardly the gaze of the tribe, to imagine its approval or reproach before acting, was an enormous advantage in a world where a misstep before the group was paid dearly. The inner spectator was born as an organ of prudence.

But that simulator does not switch off when there is no tribe. It keeps running, permanent, and projects its imaginary public onto situations where there is no one to anticipate. The group's gaze, which in its origin simulated specific people you depended on, has become an abstract and ever-present spectator, a ghost of the tribe inhabiting a mind alone in an empty room. When you fear coming off badly by refusing, by not knowing, by changing your mind, you are not reading anyone: you are consulting that simulator, and it returns to you the verdict of a tribe that no longer exists, about a scene where there is no tribe. The premium you pay is real; the counterparty that charges it is an evolutionary memory.

Refusing

Let us begin with the act that gives the chapter its name. Saying yes to what you do not want to do, out of fear, sometimes looks like a matter of pleasing another, and once in a while it is. But far more often the other expects nothing, or has not even asked with expectation; the one who says yes does so before a disapproval they have imagined in advance, that no one is issuing. You give in not to a person, but to a rule you have swallowed: that refusing is selfish, that good people do not turn others down, that a no will leave a mark. The judge who dictates that rule is internal, and its tribunal has no member but yourself.

The convex structure is here with all clarity. The cost of refusing is a brief discomfort—the other's momentary disappointment, almost always overestimated as we saw in chapter eight—bounded and passing. The gain is open and, besides, is exactly the scarcest resource you own: the time and attention you recover, which are your capital, the kind that compounds. Whoever cannot say no is bleeding their most valuable asset, drop by drop, to appease an audience that is not watching. They protect no one real; they feed a ghost with the substance of their own life.

Admitting you do not know

Saying "I don't know" costs surprisingly little in reality. People respect honest ignorance and distrust, rightly, feigned certainty; almost no one thinks worse of someone who acknowledges a limit, and they do think worse of someone caught pretending to know what they did not. The cost, then, is not charged by the world. It is charged by an image of oneself, a certain inner rank in which "I don't know" costs you points. But who keeps that ranking? No one outside. You keep it, for a judge who is you, on a leaderboard that exists only inside your head.

And again the bet is convex and rejection lets it pass. Admitting you do not know costs a blink of pride and opens an open gain: the possibility of truly learning what you did not know, the trust generated precisely by the one capable of saying it, the security of not building on a foundation of feigned knowledge that sooner or later gives way. Whoever cannot say "I don't know" shuts down learning to protect a rank no one else is scoring. They pay a very high price—staying without knowing—for a currency that has legal tender only in their private tribunal.

Changing your mind

The sharpest case is changing your mind in public when the facts change. Consistency is rewarded, or so we believe, and reversing looks like weakness, a weathervane, a lack of character. But it is worth asking who really penalizes a reversal. In the real world, the ability to update in the face of evidence is one of the most reliable marks of a serious mind, and the people whose respect is worth having respect it; those who mock whoever changes their mind are rarely judges one would want to satisfy. The one who forbids reversing is, again, the swallowed crowd, an internal auditor obsessed with appearing consistent before no one.

Here, besides, a trap appears that we already know from the mechanics under another name. Refusing to change your mind so as not to admit the previous one was wrong is honoring a sunk cost. The old belief is already paid, spent, unrecoverable; clinging to it because it cost you to adopt it is throwing good belief after bad, exactly the error that in investing ruins whoever cannot let go of a losing position.

The inner judge who demands consistency is making you hold a loss so as not to acknowledge it, which is the most expensive way to lose. Changing your mind costs the small blow of admitting you were wrong; not changing it costs staying wrong the rest of the time.

Being alone

And we arrive at the purest case of all, the one that closes the catalog because it proves the thesis beyond doubt: being alone with your own thoughts. Here there is no counterparty even in principle. There is no stranger, no public, no interlocutor. You are alone. And yet the vast majority of people do not tolerate it: the moment silence or boredom appears, the hand goes to the phone to fill the void, the same gesture as the car of the first chapter, the same flight from undivided attention of the previous chapter.

Ask where that discomfort can come from. There is no one who could be judging, because there is no one. If the unease persists in complete solitude, it can have only one source: the interior. Being alone is the act that proves, with no need for further argument, that the spectator is internal, because it is the only case in which every other possibility has been eliminated. Whoever cannot sit in silence with themselves without seeking a screen is not fleeing any external gaze; they are fleeing the ghost they carry, the simulator that keeps projecting a public even in a room where there is no one but a single person. The difficulty of being alone is the inner judge made evident, trapped in the one scene where it cannot pretend to come from outside.

What the catalog ends up revealing

Let us walk backward through what has been happening across the three directions, because the catalog, on completing itself, reveals something that was not visible at the start. Toward others, we blamed the brake on our wrong reading of the other. Toward the work, on a public that turned out to be half imaginary. And toward oneself we have arrived at acts with no other at all, where the brake remains intact. The friction, which seemed to come from outside and which we were going to be able to leave behind by changing situation, was not left behind at any station. It followed us from the full car to the empty room. And something that follows you into absolute solitude was never outside.

This forces a suspicion that the last part of the book will have to examine slowly: that the cage we have been speaking of was never the car, nor the crowd, nor the stranger. Those were occasions, not causes. The bars are internal. The judge who prevents all these acts—those directed at others and those directed at no one—is a single one, and lives inside. And if that is true, then the whole catalog begins to read differently, because these acts stop looking like techniques for extracting an advantage from an external world and begin to look like something else: blows against an inner jailer. The advantage, perhaps, was only what is seen from outside when someone dismantles those bars.

But that is too large a claim to let drop without more, and this book has no right to leap to its most flattering conclusion without first earning it. A thesis this size must first face its hardest objections: that perhaps we only hear from those who got lucky, that perhaps there are acts that are not courage but trespass, that perhaps the advantage precedes the act and not the other way around, that perhaps all of this is destroyed the moment it is done for the advantage. Before following the suspicion to the end, we must see whether it survives what can be set against it. To those cracks, and to whether the building holds despite them, the part that follows is dedicated.

PART IV

The Cracks

Chapter 11. The Thousand Emails Nobody Counts

Survivorship bias does not bring down the thesis: convexity holds it up.

Here begins the part of the book that decides whether the rest is worth anything. Until now I have built an argument and defended it; what I have not done is attack it. And an argument that only defends itself is not serious, because the seriousness of a thesis is not measured by how good it sounds when no one contradicts it, but by what remains of it when the best objections that exist are set against it. This part gathers those objections and poses them in their strongest form, without softening them, to see whether the building holds. If it does not hold, better to know it. I begin with the most obvious, the one any trained reader will have had on the tip of their tongue for several chapters now.

The objection is this. The book has been telling success stories: the cold email that changed a career, the conversation that ended in marriage, the published text that found its people. But those are the stories of the ones who won, and only them. We learn of the cold email that worked because whoever sent it got somewhere and now tells it. Of the thousand identical emails that were ignored we never learn, because those who sent them did not write memoirs about their silent failure. The graveyard does not speak. The winners write the chronicle; the losers write nothing. And therefore the whole evidentiary base of the book—"look how well these people did"—is corrupted at the root, because it comes from a sample that excludes by construction all those who failed.

An objection that knows what it is doing

It is worth not dismissing this lightly, because survivorship bias is not a vague suspicion, but one of the best-documented errors that exist, and whoever wields it here is right about how it works.

The classic example comes from the war. Military commanders examined the bombers returning from their missions and noted where they had the most bullet impacts, with the idea of armoring those areas. A statistician showed them the error: they were looking only at the planes that had come back. The ones that took hits in the truly lethal areas did not return to be examined. The armor, therefore, should not go where the surviving planes showed the most holes, but precisely where they showed none, because that was the area whose damage prevented a return. Looking only at survivors inverted the correct conclusion.

In financial markets, the same error ruins the analysis of investment results at every turn. Funds that go bust disappear from the indices, so that if you measure the performance of the funds still alive, you get an inflated figure that does not represent the strategy, but only its survivors. A track record built solely from those who survived promises returns the real strategy never delivered. And this is exactly what the objection denounces in the book: that I am measuring daring by its survivors, presenting as typical what is only what was left standing. In its harshest form, the objection adds something worse: that perhaps those who triumphed did so not by daring, but by luck, or by advantages they already carried, and that they attribute to courage what they in fact owed to a pedigree or a stroke of fortune, then write a book telling everyone to be brave. If this were true, the whole book would be a collection of planes that came back, telling how to dodge the bullets.

What exactly this objection would kill

To answer, one must be precise about what survivorship bias destroys and what it does not. What it corrupts, beyond repair, are claims about the success rate, about the typical outcome. If the book said "do these acts and you will probably triumph," the objection would tear it apart, because the visible stories would give a grossly inflated picture of the probability of triumph. Against any promise about what happens to whoever dares on average, the objection is devastating and entirely right.

But that promise is not the book's. It never was. Chapter five said, in so many words, the opposite: that these acts fail most of the time, and that it does not matter, because their rationality rests not on the hit rate but on convexity. The bet was good not because you win often, but because you lose little and bounded when you lose, which is nearly always, and win much and open the rare times you win. The objection is aiming with enormous accuracy at a claim the book not only did not make, but expressly denied.

And here the objection turns on itself, because the graveyard full of ignored emails is not a refutation of convexity: it is its prediction. A convex strategy is defined precisely by having an immense graveyard and a handful of enormous survivors. Venture capital buries the majority of its investments, and that graveyard of dead companies does not refute venture capital: it is venture capital. To reproach a convex bet for the fact that most of its attempts fail is to reproach it for being what it is. The thousand silent emails the objection exhibits as evidence for the prosecution are, exactly, what the model said would happen. They do not contradict the thesis; they confirm it to the letter.

The part of the objection that does bite

It would be dishonest to stop here, because there is a harder version of the objection that this sleight of hand does not dissolve, and the seriousness of this part of the book depends on facing it. That most fail we already conceded. But convexity is not satisfied with sometimes winning: it needs the winning tail to be big enough and frequent enough to pay for all the failures and leave the expected value positive. What if survivorship bias were inflating not the success rate, which we already discounted, but the size and frequency of that tail? What if these bets were like the lottery of chapter five, convex in form but with a secretly negative expected value, and the survivor stories made us believe the tail pays when in fact it does not? That is the real question, and it must be answered, not dodged.

The answer rests on two anchors that survivorship bias, by its very nature, cannot corrupt.

The first is the cost. To know what a rejection costs, no sample of outcomes is needed, neither survivors nor fallen: it is measured directly, by experiencing it, and it is small, brief, and certain. Survivorship bias deforms our view of the tail of gains, but does not touch the cost, which is known in advance and does not depend on whom we hear tell their story. And when the premium is so tiny and so certain, the tail need not be spectacular for the bet to pay off: it is enough that it exist, that it be barely more than zero, because the expected value is the more forgiving the cheaper the premium. The survivor stories need not be representative. The tail need only be nonzero and the cost negligible, and the second is not in doubt.

The second anchor is that the frequency of modest gains can be measured with the right kind of evidence, the kind that includes the failures. The experiments of chapter eight were not survivor anecdotes: they were controlled studies, with the complete sample, counting those who were rejected just as much as those who were attended to. And they showed that strangers are receptive far more often than we predict, that people grant a favor nearly twice as often as expected. That is, exactly, the anti-survivorship evidence: the equivalent of examining all the bombers, the fallen included, and not only the ones that came back. So we can discount to zero every spectacular anecdote, every email that changed a life, and still the bet holds, because it holds on a trivial premium and on a rate of small gains that is measured with the failures inside. The thesis did not need the dazzling survivors. It can dispense with all of them and remain standing.

What remains, and where it goes

A residue survives, and it is honest to name it. Even granting all of the above, the suspicion persists that those who triumphed did so by luck or by prior advantages, and not by daring. But that is already another objection—the one about cause and effect—and it has its own chapter a little further on, so I leave it noted there. Suffice it to say, for now, that the structural argument of the book does not depend at all on how anyone's success is attributed. It never claimed "the bold triumph because they are bold," which is a causal thesis about survivors. It claimed "the bet has a favorable structure," which is proven from the asymmetry between cost and possible gain, without reference to the causal history of any winner. The structural argument goes around the attribution problem entirely, because it does not speak of people who won, but of the shape of a bet.

So the first crack does not bring down the building. And it has done something more useful than resist: it has forced us to say precisely what the thesis rests on—on the structure, not the rate—and to realize that we have the right kind of evidence, the controlled kind that counts the failures, and not the useless kind of survivor anecdotes. The building comes out of this objection firmer than before, better founded, because it now knows exactly which stone it rests on.

There is even a hidden gift in the objection, worth collecting before we go on. Survivorship bias not only fails to refute the thesis: it helps explain why the arbitrage of chapter three does not close. If the failures are silent and the successes look like strokes of luck, then anyone trying to learn by observation whether it is worth daring receives a corrupted signal: they see a mute graveyard and a few survivors who attribute their fortune to anything but the act. The evidence in favor of the strategy is structurally hidden, and that opacity keeps the crowd away and the bill on the ground. The very bias that rose as an objection turns out to be one more reason no one comes to pick up the gain. The crack, looked at closely, was a reinforcement.

This was, besides, the kindest of the four objections, because at bottom it was about evidence, and the answer was available in the structure of the bet. The next is more uncomfortable and does not let itself be answered with a payoff diagram, because it does not ask whether the bet pays, but something different and more serious: whether there are acts that should not be done at all. Whether what I call courage may not be, at times, trespass on someone who cannot leave. That objection is not answered by calculating the return to the one who acts, because it does not speak of his gain, but of the other's cost. And to that cost, the one that does not appear on the bold person's spreadsheet, the next chapter is dedicated.

Chapter 12. The Line Between Courage and Trespass

Context, power, and consent change the calculation.

The previous crack was, at bottom, about evidence, and it closed from the structure of the bet. This one is of another nature and does not close with a payoff diagram, because it does not ask whether the act pays, but something graver: whether there are acts that should not be done at all. It is the moral objection, and it is the strongest that can be set against the book. I give it its full weight.

The objection runs thus. The book celebrates daring: speaking to strangers, approaching, initiating, asking. And it takes for granted that the cost of those acts is small and bounded. But that small and bounded cost is the cost of the one who acts. Every act directed at another person also imposes a cost on that other person, and that cost is not always small, not always bounded, and above all is not the same for everyone or in every situation. A man who approaches a woman alone on a dark street is not running the same experiment as someone who strikes up a chat in a crowded café. The woman cannot easily leave; she must reckon a threat; the "conversation" is not an offer she can decline without cost. Someone with power who approaches a subordinate is not making a bounded bet, because the subordinate cannot freely refuse. So the whole frame of the book—bounded cost, convex gain—is calculated from the sheet of the one who acts and ignores entirely the sheet of the other. And when the other's cost is returned to the account, some of these "convex bets" turn out to be predatory: the cheap option of the one who acts is written against the unconsented expense of another. "Courage" becomes a euphemism for trespass, and the book, in encouraging initiative, runs the risk of licensing precisely the conduct that makes public space unsafe for the most vulnerable.

This objection is right, and it is worth saying so plainly before qualifying anything.

The account that was missing

The core must be conceded at once, because it is true and because hiding it would be exactly the vice the objection denounces. The book's accounting, up to here, has been the actor's. I measured what it costs him to take the risk, not what it costs the other to be the object of that risk. And for any act that lands on another person, that accounting is incomplete. The convex bet was always a view from one side of the table, and a view from one side is not enough when there is someone sitting across who did not choose to play.

In the language of the book, what the objection has uncovered is an externality. The one who acts does his cost-benefit analysis, and that analysis can dump a cost on the counterparty that does not appear in the actor's books. He notes his small premium of embarrassment and his open tail of gain; he does not note, because he does not pay it, the cost he imposes on the other. And a real cost that does not figure in the account of whoever generates it, because it is suffered by a third party who did not consent, is the very definition of an externality. The question of this chapter is when these acts produce it, and where the line lies that separates legitimate initiative from imposed cost.

The variable that decides it: the costless exit

The line, it turns out, depends on a single thing, and the three variables the objection names—context, power, consent—are the three faces of that thing. What makes an act directed at another cheap and benign is not the intention of the one who acts, but that the other retain a free and costless exit. That their "no" be as cheap as your "hello."

Think of what made the café case harmless. The stranger approached can give a one-word reply, return to their book, and the interaction ends with no penalty at all for them. They have a free exit, and that is why the initiative was a benign bet: the other was never trapped. That costless exit is the entire condition for there being no externality. If the other can decline at zero cost, nothing has been imposed on them; they have been offered something they were free to refuse, and refusing cost them nothing.

Consent, then, is not a formality, but the real existence of that exit. And the other two variables are, precisely, the ones that destroy it. Power destroys it: when the one who acts has power over the other—boss and subordinate, any dependency—the other's "no" stops being free, because it is shadowed by consequences, even if nothing is explicitly threatened. The same words that between equals are a benign initiative, across a power gradient become coercive, because they have taken from the other their costless exit. And context destroys it too: the same approach carries an entirely different cost depending on who approaches whom, where, and against what background of risk. A woman approached by a strange man on an empty street must, with full rationality, run a threat calculation that a man approached by a woman in a café need not run. The context loads the other's cost to a point the actor, looking only at his own sheet, does not see. When someone says "I'm just being friendly, what's the harm?", they are doing exactly what the book condemns in all its chapters: treating their tiny premium as if it were the whole cost, when the real cost is being paid, without having consented, by another person.

It is worth noting that this is the other face of an exception I already noted. In chapter five I warned that power and context can take the ceiling off the loss, and there I said it of the actor: a joke to the boss can cost you your job, and then the bet is no longer convex for you. Here it is the same power and the same context, but seen from the other side: they take the ceiling off the other's cost. A single variable, two edges. In one case it ruins your bet; in the other, it turns your bet into a trespass.

Courage and trespass

With this, the line can be drawn clean. An act directed at another is courage—a benign convex bet—when the other can decline it freely, at zero cost, when they keep their exit. It becomes trespass when the other cannot decline without paying, because they are trapped, because there is a power gradient, or because the context forces them to reckon a threat. The variable is not daring versus timidity. It is whether the other keeps their freedom. Courage is the initiative that leaves the other free; trespass is the initiative that takes their freedom to finance your own.

And here is the important thing, the thing that keeps this concession from sinking the thesis: none of this is a moral patch brought in from outside. It is what the book's own logic demanded from the start, and only now becomes explicit. When I spoke of deadweight loss, in the chapter on the tax, the entire defense of these acts rested on their being positive for both parties: transactions where both gain, or where the other, in the worst case, suffers a trivial nuisance they were free to dodge. An act financed by the other's unconsented cost fails that condition by construction. It is not a convex bet we now, grudgingly, exclude; it is a different creature, that never met the positive-sum requirement that made these acts worth defending. The predator's cheap option is paid for by an externality it dumps on someone who did not play, and that is not arbitrage: it is extraction. The bill it picks up was not on the ground; it was in someone else's pocket. The objection, properly understood, does not contradict the thesis: it identifies acts that were never inside it.

The honest residue, and the one time the book changes its default

It would be too comfortable to end there, because the principle of the costless exit is clean in theory and treacherous in practice, for a reason that must be looked at head-on. The one who acts is a terrible judge of whether the other has a free exit or not, because he is precisely the person with the most reason to believe the exit is free. "They can say no, what's the problem?" is what the one about to impose tells himself, and also what anyone would tell themselves. The threat calculation a woman runs is not visible to the man who triggers it; he may, truly, not see it. So the principle cannot be applied by asking the actor about his intentions, because good intentions is exactly what those who trespass also report. Introspection about one's own good heart is no test.

The consequence is uncomfortable and it is inescapable. The burden falls on the one who acts, not to examine his intentions, but to read the context conservatively: to assume the other's exit is less free than it looks to him whenever there is an asymmetry of power or of threat, and to accept that, in ambiguous cases, the right course is not daring but restraint. And here happens what happens on no other page of this book: the default inverts. For eleven chapters I have defended erring toward action, because the loss was small and it was yours. In this one region, the loss is no longer small nor yours: it is, potentially, the freedom or safety of another. When the downside stops being bounded and stops being your own, the whole logic of the book turns over, and erring toward action, which has been the advice from start to finish, becomes exactly the error. Before another who may not be able to freely refuse, one errs toward restraint. This is the exception that sustains the honesty of everything else: without it, the book would be a manual for trespassers; with it, it is an argument that knows where its own jurisdiction ends.

What the exception does not touch

It matters to see that this exception, though real and grave, is narrow, because otherwise it would seem the objection carries everything off, and it does not. It applies only to acts directed at a specific other person who lacks a costless exit. It does not touch the vast majority of the catalog. It does not touch publishing, or finishing, or sustaining attention, which have no counterparty at all. It does not touch saying no, or admitting you do not know, or changing your mind, or being alone, which are directed inward. And it does not even touch much of the acts toward others, because most leave the other's exit intact. The cold email is the perfect example of an act with a free exit: the recipient has the delete key, the cheapest and most silent rejection there is, and it costs them absolutely nothing to use it. A compliment in a context where the other can go on their way, a question that can be ignored, a request that can be refused without consequence: all keep the exit, and all remain within the thesis. The region the exception carves out—approaching whoever is trapped, or under your power, or reckoning a threat—is identifiable and bounded. The book loses a corner, the corner it morally had to lose, and keeps the rest of the whole map.

What courage really was

There is one last turn, and it is the one that makes this crack, like the previous one, a reinforcement. The objection, taken seriously, reveals what the book's courage always meant. Courage was never running over another's comfort; that is not courage, it is mere force, and it is within reach of any boor willing to use it. The brave person this book praises faces their own fear and leaves the other whole. There is the distinction that sustains the chapter: courage spends one's own discomfort; trespass spends the other's freedom. The bully who corners someone is not demonstrating the virtue of this book, but its exact opposite, because his daring consumes another's freedom instead of spending only his own embarrassment. The whole book is about paying a premium that is yours to gain something you take from no one. The moment the premium is paid by another against their will, you have stopped playing this game and started playing another, much older and much uglier.

Two cracks remain. We have seen whether the bet pays, and we have seen whether it should be done. The next question is more slippery than both, because it attacks neither the return nor the morality of the act, but its cause. It suspects we have inverted the order: that perhaps it is not the act that produces the advantage, but that only those who already have advantage, security, position, can afford the act. If that were true, the whole book would be useless advice, addressed to those who need it least and barred to those who need it most. To that suspicion, the chicken and the egg, the next chapter is dedicated.

Chapter 13. The Chicken or the Egg?

Cause and effect feed each other, but the act is the way into the circle.

The two previous cracks attacked the return of the act and its morality. This one attacks something prior to both: its cause. And it is more slippery, because it does not deny that the bold do well; it denies that they do well because they are bold. It suspects we have inverted the entire order of the book.

The objection unfolds on three fronts, and it is worth seeing them separately because they are not the same. The first is reversed causation: perhaps it is not that the act produces the advantage, but the reverse, that only those who already have advantage—a stable position, social capital, a network that sustains them, a temperament without wounds—can afford the act. Confidence would not be what you do, but what you can afford to do. The second front is confounding: perhaps a third variable—a comfortable background, inherited security, a fortunate temperament—produces both the daring and the prosperity, so that the correlation between act and success is spurious, and neither causes the other. And the third front, the one that would really do damage, is moral. If either of the first two is true, the book's advice is not only false: it is cruelly false. Useless for those who most need it, the insecure, those with no network, because they cannot afford the act; and redundant for those who least need it, the already secure, who were going to be fine anyway. The book would be teaching the drowning person to swim by describing the technique of those standing on dry land. It would be a class artifact disguised as universal advice, the comfortable congratulating themselves on virtues that were in fact privileges.

This objection is strong, and the third part is the one that must really be answered, because the first two could be true without the book collapsing, but the third, if it holds, condemns it entirely.

Yes, there is a loop

The true part must be conceded at once, and it is considerable. The relationship between security and the act is not a clean arrow in a single direction. Security does make the act cheaper: for someone with a net beneath them, taking a risk costs less, because a fall does not destroy them. And the act does build security: every time you dare and it goes well, or simply does not go badly, the next daring weighs less. It is a loop, a circle that feeds itself, and to pretend the cause runs only from act to advantage would be dishonest and also false.

In markets, this phenomenon has been given a name: reflexivity. The idea that the perception of the participants and the reality they perceive are not separated by an arrow, but joined by a loop, where what people believe moves prices, and the moved prices alter the fundamentals people believed they were reading. Perception and reality manufacture each other. Confidence and outcome, in our subject, do exactly that: they co-produce. Whoever believes themselves capable acts, and in acting becomes more capable, which confirms that they believed themselves capable. There is no clean first link. Conceded, whole, without haggling.

But a loop has two doors

And yet conceding the loop does not concede the objection, because the objection needs more than a loop: it needs the arrow to run in a single direction, from advantage to act, leaving the act as a mere symptom with no causal power of its own. And that is false, for a reason that lies in the very nature of a loop.

A feedback loop has no mandatory entry node. You can enter through either of the two. The objection takes for granted that you can only enter through security: first become secure, and then you will be able to act. But you also enter through the act: act first, and security comes behind, which makes the next act cheaper, which builds more security. The circle does not require starting on one side. And here is the decisive thing: of the two nodes, only one is available at will. You cannot decide to feel secure. Security is, in large measure, a result, a downstream state, an output of the system, not a lever you can pull by decree. No one has become secure by deciding to. But you can decide to perform the act, right now, with whatever security you have, because the act—we already established this in chapter three—requires no capital, no credential, no prior position; its means are distributed universally and for free. So, even granting the whole loop, the act is the only door the will can open. "Become secure first" is not actionable advice, because no one knows how to execute a state. "Act" is. The book points to the only node of the loop a person can actually touch.

Why the door opens precisely to the insecure

Now the moral sting, which is where the objection believed it had its best blow, and where it is turned around. The objection holds that the act is only affordable for whoever has a net. But the whole book, in its fourth and fifth chapters, established the opposite: that the cost of the act is bounded and tiny, a few seconds of social discomfort. And a net beneath matters when the fall is big. When the fall is small by construction, when the downside is already on the floor, there is nothing for the net to catch, and the net becomes irrelevant. You do not need a cushion to survive an ignored email, because there is no blow to soften.

This means the act is not paid for with reserves of security, but with a different currency: courage, denominated in seconds of embarrassment. And that currency is not distributed by class. The person with no security whatsoever sends the cold email at the same tiny cost as the person with every advantage, because neither of them pays it from a fund of inherited position; both pay it from the same handful of uncomfortable seconds, a currency everyone holds equally. Far from being the privilege the objection denounces, the act is, probably, the least privilege-dependent lever there is, precisely because its entry price is denominated in something class does not distribute. Compare it with the routes that do demand prior advantage—capital, credentials, the network one is born into: those are indeed barred to whoever lacks them. The bold act is the exception, the only route upward whose toll is not a privilege. It is the fire escape for whoever has the main gate shut.

The confounding is real, but it proves inequality, not uselessness

The part of the objection that does bite remains, and it must be conceded precisely. It is true that part of what looks like "daring pays" is confounded: the well-connected person's cold email lands in part because of who they are, not only because they sent it. The returns are confounded and unequal. The advantaged one gets a fatter tail from the same act, because their gains compound on a larger base, as we saw in the chapter on compound interest.

But notice what that proves exactly. It proves the returns are unequal, not that the act is useless. And sharpening what we already said in the survivorship crack: the book's claim was never "daring causes success," which is a thesis about outcomes and therefore vulnerable to confounding. It was "the act has a favorable structure," which is a property of the bet and not of who makes it. The asymmetry between bounded cost and open gain belongs to the act, not the actor. The advantaged one will have a wider tail; but the disadvantaged one faces the same bounded cost and nonzero gain, which is all convexity requires. The confounding changes the size of the tail between one person and another; it does not change the sign of the bet for anyone. The returns are unequal, true, but an index fund returns less in absolute terms to the poor investor than to the rich one, and it does not thereby stop being the best vehicle available to the poor one. The act returns less to whoever has less base, and it remains, even so, the highest-return lever that person can reach, and the only one that does not demand the base they do not have.

The loop that traps, unsweetened

It would be easy to stay in the optimistic version of the loop, and it would be dishonest, because the loop also runs in the opposite direction and can trap. For whoever has little security, the circle turns vicious: the little security makes the felt cost of the act heavier—the fear tax of chapter four is progressive against whoever has less margin—so they act less, build less security, and the act keeps seeming expensive. The loop can pin someone to the bottom, and there is no pretending otherwise.

But even this, looked at closely, does not rescue the objection, but locates precisely where the lever is. If the loop can be entered through the act node, then the highest-leverage intervention for someone trapped at the bottom is exactly to perform the act despite the heavier felt cost, because it is the only move capable of flipping the circle from vicious to virtuous. And there is a detail that changes everything: the heavier felt cost is not a heavier real cost. The real cost of the act remains bounded and tiny for everyone; what is greater in the insecure person is the felt premium, the price their fear charges them. And chapter six already taught us what to do with the felt premium: it is the output of a miscalibrated model, a ghost, something to be worked around and not obeyed. So the insecure person's larger fear is not evidence that the act costs them more in truth; it is the old model charging them a higher phantom premium, which is precisely what one must place a calculation ahead of in order to ignore. The advice is not "this is easy." The advice is "this is the lever, it is the only one you can reach, and the extra fear you feel is an imaginary price, not a real one."

What remains standing

Recapping honestly what was conceded and what was defended: the causality is reflexive, a loop and not an arrow, and security and the act co-produce. Conceded. The returns are confounded and unequal, and the advantaged one gets more from the same act. Conceded. The loop can turn vicious and trap whoever starts with less. Conceded. But from none of these three truths does what the objection needed follow: that the act is useless, or that the cause runs only from advantage to act. The act is the entry door to the loop; it is the accessible door, the only one the will opens; and it is the least dependent on prior advantage there is, because it is paid in a currency class does not distribute.

A loop that feeds itself is, after all, a process that compounds, and compounding needs a first deposit. The advantaged one inherits a principal to start from. Whoever inherits nothing has one single way to make the first deposit: the act, paid with the only currency they already possess without anyone having given it to them. The book is not, then, those on dry land describing the stroke to the one drowning. It is the only instruction that names the only lever reachable without having been saved first.

Three cracks are closed and one, the last, is the strangest of all, because it does not come from outside the thesis: it comes from inside. The three previous ones attacked the bet from without—its evidence, its morality, its cause. The last suspects the building sabotages itself. That in the very instant you perform these acts for the advantage that thirteen chapters have been calculating, you destroy the only thing that produced the value. That this arbitrage, unlike all the others, does not survive being treated as an arbitrage. To that paradox, the one that bites its own tail, the chapter that closes the cracks is dedicated.

Chapter 14. The Arbitrage That Destroys Itself

It pays only with sincerity: to instrumentalize it corrupts it.

The three previous cracks attacked the thesis from outside: they doubted its evidence, its morality, its cause. In all three cases the building held. This last one is of another species, because it does not come from outside. It comes from within, from the very heart of the thesis, and it suspects the book sabotages itself. It is the deepest objection, and I say from the start that I will not refute it, because it is true. What I will do is follow it to the end, because its truth, carried to where it leads, does not destroy the book: it pushes it beyond itself.

The objection runs thus. All these acts derive their value from sincerity. The conversation with the stranger creates a bond because it is a real human opening, not a transaction. The compliment lands because it is felt, not because it is calculated. The cold email works when it is genuine interest, not a networking maneuver. Gratitude moves because it is real gratitude. But the book has dedicated thirteen chapters to teaching you to see these acts as convex bets, to calculate their expected value, to pursue the advantage. And in the very instant you perform the act with that frame switched on—"I speak to this person because it is a positive-value bet on my network"—you have turned it into a transaction, and the other perceives it, and the sincerity that produced the value has vanished. The instrumentalized compliment is not a compliment: it is flattery, and it repels. The calculated opening is not a bond: it is extraction, and people smell it. So the book's frame, if it is really applied at the moment of acting, poisons the well. It is a recipe that stops working the moment it is consciously followed. And this is worse than the previous objections, because it means the book is self-destructive by design: the more you internalize its thesis, the worse you perform the acts. A perfect student of this book would be a worse conversationalist, a more transparent flatterer, a more repellent contact, than someone who never read it. The knowledge poisons itself.

It is true, and it has a name

One must not resist this, because it is true, and resisting would be the error. It must be conceded whole and with precision, because in the precision lies the way out.

There exists a whole class of things that cannot be reached by aiming at them directly. Sleep is the clearest: you cannot resolve to sleep; the very attempt to sleep keeps you awake. Spontaneity is the same: the moment you seek it, it stops being spontaneous. A philosopher called these states that are essentially by-products, states that only arrive as a side effect of actions undertaken for another reason, and that evaporate the moment they are made the goal. Human connection is one of them. Admiration, trust, affection: all flee the hand that grabs them.

Economics has its own version of this law, and it is exact. When a measure becomes a target, it ceases to be a good measure. In the instant the by-product—the bond, the advantage—becomes the target the act aims at, the act stops producing it. It is Goodhart's law applied to the soul. Connection was the measure that the act was sincere; make it the target, and the act stops being sincere, and therefore stops producing connection. The objection, at bottom, is pointing at this: that aiming at the advantage dissolves it.

And it is entirely right. Reaching your hand toward the payoff, closing it around the payoff, is exactly what makes it disappear.

What this establishes exactly, and what it does not

Here one must be surgical, because everything depends on the distinction. That aiming at the payoff dissolves it establishes one very precise thing: that the payoff cannot be the operative reason at the moment of acting. It does not establish that the payoff is not real. It does not establish that the bet is not convex. These are entirely different claims, and confusing them is what makes the objection seem to sink the book.

The advantage is still there. The expected value is still positive. The bet is still convex. The only thing the paradox proves is that this payoff can be received, but not grabbed. It is like the astronomer's peripheral vision: there are stars so faint that they are seen only by looking slightly to one side; if you fix your gaze directly on them, they disappear, not because they are not there, but because of how seeing works. The advantage is one of those stars. It is in the sky, it is real, and only whoever is not looking at it head-on collects it.

And it is worth specifying, so as not to betray the whole thesis of the book: this does not mean the arbitrage closes. The bill is still on the ground, as always, with no one picking it up; the opportunity remains open. What fails is not the opportunity, but the gesture of grabbing it as an opportunity. The hand that closes on the advantage closes on nothing. The bill is still there, intact, for the hand that was not trying to grab it.

The two levels

The paradox dissolves entirely as soon as two things the objection keeps glued together are separated: the justification of a practice and the motive within a concrete act of that practice.

The reason it is worth cultivating the practice of sincere connection—its justification—can perfectly well be the enormous value it returns over a life. But the motive you must hold while performing an act of that practice—your operative reason in the instant—cannot be that value: it has to be the sincere giving itself. And these two do not contradict each other, because they live on different levels. You can believe, at the level of reflection, that speaking to strangers is a convex bet of positive value, and at the same time give yourself, at the level of action, purely for the human contact, with no thought of return whatsoever. The reflective belief is what gets you into the room; sincerity is what governs how you are once inside. The book operates at the first level: it explains why it is worth cultivating the practice. It never asked you to run the expected-value calculation during the conversation. To ask that would be, indeed, to poison the well; but the book never asked it, and the objection attributes to it an instruction it did not give.

So the frame is not self-destructive. It is self-erasing, which is different. It is a frame that, properly understood, instructs you to let it go at the moment of acting. It tells you: understand that this pays, let that understanding move you to do it, and then, in doing it, forget it. There is no contradiction in a map that takes you to the door and asks you to put it away before entering.

What the resolution forces us to admit

But following the paradox to the end forces us to admit something more, and that something more is the door to the rest of the book. If the payoff is received only through sincere giving, and sincerity cannot be faked—a faked sincerity is just instrumentalization with a mask, detectable as we saw in chapter eight, and it fails all the same—then the only stable way to collect this by-product across an entire life is not to learn to act as if you were sincere. It is to become, in truth, the kind of person for whom these acts are sincere. Someone who speaks to the stranger because people make them curious. Who praises because they notice and appreciate. Who asks because they trust. Who publishes because they have something to say.

And at that point, notice, the frame of advantage has consumed itself in silence. Because that person no longer does these acts for the advantage. They do them because they are who they are. The advantage still comes to them—the by-product still lands, the faint star is still in the sky—but it has become genuinely incidental, the side effect of a way of being instead of a pursued goal. The calculation did its work and disappeared, leaving in its place not a more skillful calculator, but someone who no longer needs to calculate.

The ladder

This is the conclusion the whole book was working toward, and it is beautiful that it arrives here, as the resolution of its own deepest objection. The logic of advantage, followed to the end, dissolves itself and deposits you somewhere else. It tells you: pursue the payoff. But the payoff is received only with sincerity. But sincerity cannot be faked. But the only reliable way to sustain sincerity for a whole life is to become someone for whom these acts are ends in themselves. And that someone no longer pursues the payoff. Each step of the reasoning is correct, and the whole leads you, step by step, to abandon the starting point.

The frame of arbitrage is, then, a ladder. It serves to let you see the structure, it moves you to change, and then, at the very top, it is kicked away, because the person it has turned you into no longer needs or uses it. You climb an argument about advantage and arrive at a place where advantage is beside the point. The self-destruction of this arbitrage is not a defect of the book: it is the mechanism by which the book delivers you beyond its own frame. The three previous cracks had to be sealed for the building to stay standing. This one did not have to be sealed. It had to be walked through, because it was a door.

What lies on the other side

With this the four cracks are closed, and in a way worth noticing. The first three were answered from outside and discarded: the building withstood the attacks. The fourth was not discarded; it was conceded, and its concession turned out to be the threshold. The book has thus earned the right to say aloud what it barely dared to hint at the end of the catalog: that these acts were never, really, about the advantage. The advantage was real, yes, but it was the shadow, the observable trace something else leaves as it passes. For thirteen chapters we measured it, calculated it, pursued it, and that work was necessary, because only by pursuing it to the end does one discover that it dissolves between the fingers and that behind it there was something else.

Now, with the frame of arbitrage set aside at the top of its own ladder, we can at last look head-on at that something else. Recall what the catalog left us suspecting: that the cage was never outside, that these acts were blows against an inner jailer, that what we were doing all along, without naming it, was freeing ourselves. The advantage was the proof that freedom works, but it was not freedom. The part that follows stops measuring the shadow and turns toward what casts it. It no longer asks how much daring returns, but what it is, really, that had us tied; and why leaving there is not just a good deal, but something older and graver, that has to do with ceasing to fear other people. To that, to the exit, the last part of the book is dedicated.

PART V

The Exit

Chapter 15. It Wasn't an Advantage, It Was a Cage

They were not techniques, but the conduct of someone who does not fear judgment.

For fourteen chapters, the advantage was the figure and freedom was the ground. We looked at the advantage—measured it, calculated it, pursued it—and freedom stayed behind, unnamed, like the backdrop no one speaks of because no one sees it. The previous chapter inverted that relationship without quite saying so: it showed that the advantage dissolves when grabbed, and that it arrives only as a by-product of a way of being. If that is true, then the way of being is the real subject, and the advantage was merely its trace. This chapter makes the inversion explicit. It stops looking at the shadow and turns toward what casts it.

And what casts it has a simple name. All the acts of the catalog—speaking to strangers, asking, thanking, publishing, finishing, saying no, admitting you do not know, being alone—are what a person who does not fear the judgment of others does, effortlessly and as one breathes. They are not techniques that person deploys. They are symptoms of what that person is. No one who is free needs to be taught to "speak to strangers as a convex bet"; they simply speak to strangers, because nothing stops them. The acts were not optimization tools a book could hand you. They were the description, seen from outside, of how someone behaves who is no longer bound by the fear of being watched.

One cage, one key

The book has described many acts and many barriers, and it might seem you need to master a hundred distinct skills. But chapter ten had already begun to collapse them into one, and now the inversion completes it. There was never a plurality of barriers—shyness on one side, fear of rejection on another, resistance to publishing on a third. There was a single barrier with many disguises: the fear of being judged. Every unperformed act of the catalog, without exception, refers back to it. You stay quiet in the car out of fear of judgment. You do not ask out of fear of judgment.

You do not publish, do not correct yourself, do not say no, all from the same root, dressed each time as something else.

And if there is a single barrier, there is also a single key. A hundred techniques are not needed, because there are not a hundred locks: there is one, and all the acts of the catalog hang from it. Ceasing to fear judgment opens, all at once, the door to all of them, not because you have learned a hundred skills, but because the one thing that kept them all shut has been withdrawn. That is why this could be a book and not a list of tips. A list enumerates a hundred remedies for a hundred ills. A book can afford a single thesis because it has seen that the hundred ills are one, and that the hundred remedies are, at bottom, the same gesture repeated: letting go of the same fear.

Why we had to speak of advantage

One might reasonably ask whether the thirteen chapters of advantage were then a deception, a bait to sell something else. They were not, and the previous chapter already gave one reason: the ladder had to be climbed in order to be set aside. But there is one more reason, and it is worth stating, because it explains the whole architecture of the book.

The language of advantage was the only one that could reach someone still inside the cage. To a person who fears judgment, telling them "stop fearing judgment, it is a cage" is of no use: either it means nothing, or it terrifies them, because it asks them to let go of precisely what they feel as their security. But telling them "there is free money on the ground and you are leaving it there" is legible; it speaks to the part of them that is not yet free, the part that calculates, and it manages to move them to take the first step. And the first step, taken sincerely, begins to dissolve the fear from within, through the reflexive loop we saw. The advantage was not a trick. It was the handhold. You reach a frightened person through their self-interest, and their self-interest, followed to the end, delivers them beyond self-interest. The vocabulary of the cage served to speak to them and to get them out of it.

What the cage was, said without calculation

Now it can be named without the financial scaffolding, because the scaffolding has already done its job and can be set down. The cage was the fear of others' judgment. And, as chapter ten showed, above all the judgment of an internalized, imaginary tribunal, a jury we carry with us that delivers verdicts in the name of a crowd that is not even watching.

It is a cage for three reasons, and it is worth seeing them together. First: it constrains you far more than any external force. No one really stops you from speaking, publishing, asking; there is no guard, no wall, no law. The bars are entirely internal, and that is why they are more effective than any grate, because a grate can be forced and these bars obey on their own. Second: it is a cage whose door was never locked. You were free to leave the whole time. There lies its particular cruelty and also its particular hope: no one locked you in, you stayed. Third, and the most expensive: it costs you your life, in the exact sense established by the chapter on compound interest. Not just any life, but an entire life of bonds and work that compound, surrendered not to any jailer, but to a ghost. Whoever lives in this cage pays, for decades, an enormous ransom to a kidnapper who does not exist.

The inversion

With this, the whole proposal of the book turns over, and it is worth stating the inversion cleanly, because the order is everything.

The book seemed to say: here are valuable acts; do them to gain an advantage. What it really says is: here is a single cage; leave it, and these acts will come on their own, and the advantage will come behind them, without your calling it. The order matters all the way down. You do not do the acts in order to become free; you become free and the acts do themselves. The advantage is not the goal you pursue by executing the catalog; freedom is the state from which the catalog springs, and the advantage merely accumulates on top, like a residue. If one last financial image serves before we put it away for good, it is this: freedom is the asset, and the advantage is the dividend that asset pays out. You spent the whole time trying to buy the dividend directly, which is impossible, when the only thing one can own is the asset, and the dividend comes, automatic, to whoever owns it. Stop chasing the payout and tend to the asset, and the payout will take care of itself.

What it is not, and what it is

Here one must stop and be honest, because "stop fearing judgment" threatens to become another useless piece of advice, of the kind we already rejected. You cannot decide to feel free, just as you could not decide to feel secure or fake sincerity. Freedom, like everything valuable in this book, is also a by-product, and is not reached by aiming at it head-on. Does that not leave us empty-handed?

No, and here the whole structure of the book yields its fruit. It is true you cannot want freedom directly. But you can want the one thing that does let itself be wanted: the act, despite the fear. And one must be precise about what the act achieves, because chapter six forbade us an illusion. That chapter made clear that the alarm of fear does not switch off: you can prove it wrong a thousand times and it will sound again the thousand-and-first, because it does not learn at your pace. So freedom is not, cannot be, the absence of fear. That was never on offer. Freedom is something else, more modest and more powerful: it is the revocation of fear's authority. The judge keeps speaking; you stop obeying it. You do not stop feeling watched; you stop obeying the watcher. You keep hearing the alarm, and you act anyway, knowing it is an old detector howling at burnt toast and not a verdict to be carried out.

And that revocation is reached through the act. Every time you act despite the fear, you do not silence the alarm, but you strip it of a little of its command, because you verify once more that the feared judge was a ghost, that the star was not where you looked at it head-on. The road to freedom, which cannot be wanted, runs through the act, which can. The book does not ask you to feel free. It asks you to act as if the judge were not there, again and again, and to let the acting teach the feeling who is in charge.

Why a good deal is not enough

There remains, however, a question the book has been circling and can no longer postpone. We have said why it is worth revoking fear's authority: because obeying it costs an entire life that compounds. But that is still the language of advantage, and we have climbed beyond advantage. It is a prudential reason, a good-deal reason, and there is something unsatisfying about founding freedom on profitability, as if being free were worth it only because it pays.

One may suspect there is a deeper reason. That subordinating your conduct to the crowd's judgment is not merely unprofitable, but wrong. That it is an error not only of accounting, but of orientation: an error about what a human being owes, and to whom. Here the book's argument has to stop being economic and become moral, because the question is no longer how much the cage costs, but why it is unworthy to live in it. And the answer has to do with something no spreadsheet records: that subordinating one's own conduct to the crowd's judgment is a form of servitude, and of the worst kind, because no one imposes it on us. It is a chain we hold with our own hand, and to surrender out of fear the authorship of one's own life to a tribunal that never had the right to judge it is not just a bad deal: it is an abdication. To that reason, the one that speaks not of return but of dignity, the next chapter is dedicated.

Chapter 16. The Judge We Crowned

To obey the judgment of others is not merely unprofitable: it is a servitude one imposes on oneself.

The previous chapter ended on a dissatisfaction, and it was an honest one. We had given a reason to leave the cage: that staying inside costs an entire life that compounds. But that is the language of advantage, and the whole book had come precisely from discovering that advantage was the shadow and not the thing. To found freedom on profitability has something contradictory about it: it would be leaving the cage for a good deal, when what the book has been revealing is that the cage itself is the problem, whatever price is paid for it. A reason is needed that does not speak of return. A reason that says not that fearing the crowd's judgment is unprofitable, but that it is wrong.

Here the book abandons entirely the financial vocabulary that sustained it until now, because the argument it needs is no longer economic. And the question changes in nature. It stops being how much the cage costs and becomes another, more uncomfortable: whose life is being lived inside it. Because the accusation of this chapter, the one that turns an inefficiency into a moral error, is that whoever lives governed by what people will say is not, in a precise sense, living their own life.

Who the author is

Consider what it means, exactly, to subordinate your conduct to the judgment of others. It means that the question "what will I do?" is answered by consulting "what will they think?" And that amounts to handing the authorship of your own acts to other people. Not to one, but to a diffuse and imaginary crowd, as we saw: a jury you carry inside that rules in the name of people who are not even watching. Whoever lives this way does not decide; they consult. They do not act from their own reasons, but from the forecast of others' approval. Their life is written, in practice, by people who are not them, who never accepted the charge of directing it, and who will never answer for how it turns out.

This can be called many things, but the most exact is abdication. One abdicates the one thing that is, truly, inalienably one's own: the authorship of one's own conduct. Everything else can be lost or ceded—goods, position, even physical freedom—but the faculty of deciding what to do with what falls to you is the core of being a person, and it is what is given away here. And here is the reason it is a moral error and not a mere practical misstep: the capacity to govern oneself is not useful, it is constitutive. It is what makes someone an agent and not just an object moved by forces. A being who acts solely out of fear of others' judgment is doing neither good nor evil; they are not, strictly, acting: they are being pushed. So subordination to what people will say is not one vice among others. It is a fault at the very root of moral life, because it corrodes the condition without which there is no conduct to judge: that the conduct be yours.

No one forces us

It might be objected that abdicating something imposed on you carries neither merit nor blame; that if the crowd forces us, we are not guilty of submitting. And it would be a comfortable way out if it were true. It is not, and what makes it false is the most important observation of this chapter: no one forces us.

Almost five centuries ago, a young magistrate wrote a brief and furious text on why peoples tolerate tyrants. His answer was not the fear of force, but something more disturbing: that servitude is, at bottom, voluntary. The tyrant has no more power than his subjects lend him; the day they stopped obeying, with no need to rise up, merely by withdrawing their consent, the tyrant would fall on his own. What sustains domination is not the chain, it is the hand that holds it from within. And what was scandalous, to that author, was that men not only consent to their subjection, but often defend it and love it, handing over their freedom in exchange for nothing.

The cage of this book is exactly that: a voluntary servitude. We had already said it another way, in noting that the door was never locked. No one forces you to obey the imaginary jury. There is no guard, no law, no real punishment that falls on whoever stops consulting the crowd before acting. The chain is held by you, and you could let it go at any moment. And it is precisely that voluntariness that turns misfortune into fault. A servitude you can end whenever you want, and do not end, is a servitude you are choosing. You are not, then, the victim of the crowd. You are its collaborator. The jailer whose salary you pay is yourself, and the life you do not live is taken from you by no one: you hand it over.

The alibi

This is hard to acknowledge, and for a reason that aggravates the error instead of excusing it. We almost never tell ourselves the truth about what we do. In yielding to what people will say, we do not call it fear or submission; we call it prudence, courtesy, humility, consideration for others, common sense. We dress abdication in the garb of a virtue so as not to have to see it. Whoever does not say what they think tells themselves they are discreet; whoever does not do what they want, that they are responsible; whoever bends, that they are mature. And sometimes those words are true, because prudence and courtesy exist. But with enormous frequency they are alibis, decorous names for the same old act: the fear of judgment, disguised as something we can respect in the mirror.

Here the moral error folds over on itself. Not only do we abdicate the authorship of our life; we also lie to ourselves about having done so. And the lie to oneself is the most expensive of all, because it poisons the faculty with which one might, someday, correct oneself. Whoever calls their cowardice a virtue has shut from within the door that not even the crowd had shut, because they no longer see it as a door. The first step toward leaving is not becoming brave; it is ceasing to lie to yourself about why you stay.

It is not answering to no one

Arriving here, a misunderstanding lurks that must be defused, because it is the trap almost everyone falls into who tries to free themselves from what people will say by the easy route. One might believe the solution is simply to stop answering to anyone: that to be free is to care nothing for others' opinion, to do whatever you please, to treat your own whim as law. That is not freedom. It is another form of slavery, and sometimes worse, because a person who answers to nothing does not govern themselves: they are governed by their impulses, which are as external to their reflective will as the crowd. Either they deceive themselves, and go on secretly performing for some gallery, smaller or more select, but a gallery all the same. Or they are left adrift, with no measure by which the word "right" could even mean anything.

The true exit is not to answer to no one, but to answer to a tribunal higher than the crowd. And that tribunal, stripped of all mysticism, is your own conscience: your examined reasons, your defensible convictions, your considered idea of what is worth doing. You do not free yourself from others' judgment by declaring yourself king of yourself, because a self that obeys only its own whim is merely another tyrant, and a fickle one at that. You free yourself when you become capable of giving yourself a law you can sustain with arguments, one that answers to what you truly believe and not to what you fear they will think. Then the crowd loses its authority, not because you have stopped being accountable, but because you have begun to be accountable to an instance that does have jurisdiction over your life—you, reasoning honestly—rather than one that never had it: the opinion of people who have not devoted a single minute to thinking about your case. The inner judge we spoke of does not fall silent; it goes on ruling. But you take back the crown you had placed on it, and give it to another judge, one that does have the right to wear it.

The first thing of all

Notice that this is not one virtue among many, but the condition of all the others. A person still governed by the fear of judgment cannot, however much they want to, reliably do good, for a simple and relentless reason: the right and the approved do not always coincide, and whoever fears will always choose the approved. As long as the crowd's verdict has the last word, the last word will never belong to your conscience. You cannot be honest if honesty exposes you to disapproval and you cannot bear disapproval. You cannot be just, or brave, or kind when kindness costs, until you have stopped needing others' permission to act. That is why freedom from what people will say is the ground on which any other good thing you want to do is built. Remove that ground, and all the virtues you thought you had turn out to be conditional on no one looking at you badly, which is to say you do not have them.

The two halves

With this the book has, at last, its two halves complete. The prudential: staying in the cage costs a life that compounds. And the moral: staying in the cage is an abdication, a servitude one imposes on oneself, the surrender of the authorship of one's own life to a tribunal that never had the right to judge it. The first appeals to your interest; the second, to your dignity. And they do not contradict each other, because they are, again, two levels of a single truth, as the justification and the motive were in the chapter on the arbitrage that destroys itself. The advantage brings you to the door; dignity tells you why to cross it even if there were no advantage at all.

Everything the book had to argue is now said. The structure of the phenomenon, its mechanics, its catalog, its cracks, its exit. Only one thing is missing, and it is not a new argument, but a return. We began in a silent car, watching a person who spoke while the others stayed quiet, and we used that scene as the cleanest case of everything that would come. It is worth going back to it now, at the end, and seeing it again with everything we know, because the whole book fits, compressed, into that minimal and everyday gesture, and only at the end can one fully understand what was really happening when someone, in a car full of mute people, decided to speak.

Chapter 17. The Car, Again

Freedom as the conclusion: the advantage was only its observable proof.

Let us go back to the car we began with. Not to add an argument—everything that had to be argued is already said—but to read, now that we know all we know, what was really happening in that minimal gesture we used, at the start, as the cleanest case of everything that would come. I said in the first chapter that it was not a scene but a natural experiment, and that its virtue was to repeat itself identically thousands of times a day. It is time to see what that experiment was really measuring.

Thirty people in a few square meters, twenty-nine quiet, one who speaks. Let us follow that single person, the one who breaks the pact of silence, and unfold, layer by layer, everything that is true of her in the instant she opens her mouth.

The whole book in one gesture

She is, without knowing it, picking up a twenty that has been lying on the floor of every crowded space since crowded spaces have existed. She is taking an arbitrage that does not close, one of those that competition should have swept up centuries ago and that remains intact, car after car, generation after generation. She is doing nothing hard: the means to do it were distributed among the thirty equally, free and complete. She is, simply, one of the few who paid the tiny internal toll the other twenty-nine refused.

In doing so, she has overcome a tax. Fear inflated her premium, discounted at a usurious rate any future benefit, erased from the books what it could not see in advance, and offered her silence with the misleading label of free. She paid anyway, a few seconds of discomfort sunk into the act itself, and bought with them a convex option: bounded loss, open gain. And it does not matter—this is what almost no one understands—that this particular conversation, in all likelihood, leads nowhere. The bet was good by its shape, not by its result, and a bet good by its shape is judged in the aggregate of a life, never in the isolated attempt.

She has acted, besides, against an alarm that will never fall silent, a risk model calibrated for a tribe that vanished millennia ago and that still treats a stranger's gaze as a mortal threat. She did not silence it: that was not on offer. She revoked its authority. She heard the howl of the old detector and spoke anyway. And if she does this not once but as a way of being in the world, the minuscule gesture will compound over the years until it becomes something that, seen from outside, will look like luck, or a gift, or a talent she lacks as much as anyone. It will be none of the three. It will be a small rate, sustained, in the exponent of time.

She has corrected, in that same act, the wrong portrait she made of the other: she will discover, almost always, that the stranger did not want to be left alone as much as she feared. And if she is capable of doing this even when no one is watching, even alone with herself, then she has begun to dethrone the judge she carried inside, the ghost that delivered verdicts in the name of a crowd that was not even looking at her.

Her act, besides, survives everything that can be set against it. It is not a survivor's mirage, because it rests on the structure of the bet and not on the anecdotes of those who won. It is not a trespass, because the other keeps his exit whole: a dry word, the return to the book, and the interaction ends at no cost to him. It is not the privilege of one who was already secure, because the toll she paid was not denominated in capital or position, but in courage, a currency class does not distribute. And it does not matter that she cannot do it "for the advantage," because the only act that pays is the sincere one, and she is not calculating: she is, simply, speaking.

What we were looking at

With all the layers gathered, the question the book opened with has at last its complete answer. What were we looking at, in that car, when someone spoke?

Not a shrewd person taking advantage. All the apparatus we have used to understand her—the arbitrage, the convexity, the tax, the compound interest, the phantom counterparty, the externality—was scaffolding, a borrowed tool for seeing the structure of something that at bottom was not a financial operation. We can now, for the last time, set all those tools on the ground, because the building they held up is standing and we can see it whole without them. What we were looking at was, simply, a free person being free. A person who had stopped obeying a fear that lied to her, and who therefore did, naturally, what almost no one does, not because she had learned a technique, but because she no longer carried what bound the others.

And the advantage—the friendship that might come, the door that might open, the life that might change—was never the object. It was the shadow. It was the observable trace freedom leaves as it passes, the one thing in all this that could be measured from outside, and that is why it was what we measured, chapter after chapter, with all the rigor we could muster. We measured the shadow because the shadow lets itself be measured. But the person who cast it was not working for the shadow. She was free, and the advantage fell where the free walk, without her pursuing it. That is, exactly, the conclusion of the book: the advantage was the observable proof that freedom works. Not its prize, not its end. Its proof.

The door that was never locked

One turn remains, and it is toward the reader. The other twenty-nine people in the car, the ones who stay quiet, are not villains. They are us, almost always, obeying a fear we now understand completely: its ancient origin, its miscalibrated logic, its inflated premium, and the voluntary servitude it hid. We must not despise them. We must recognize ourselves in them. The car, besides, was never really about meters or about conversations with strangers; it was the cleanest case of a situation that repeats in every room, every inbox, every blank page, every moment when something small and valuable is a gesture away and a fear that lies tells us no.

And over that car, over every car, weighs a single fact that changes everything and that it is fitting to end on. The door was never locked. No one locked the twenty-nine in. There was no guard, no grate, no law; only a toll of a few seconds of embarrassment that almost everyone, almost always, refused to pay, convinced by an alarm that did not tell the truth that on the other side there was a danger. On the other side there was no danger. There was another person, and a whole life of people, and works, and doors, waiting on the open side of a door that only seemed closed.

It took seventeen chapters and a whole apparatus borrowed from finance to say what that person said, in the first car, with a single sentence addressed to a stranger.

That fear was lying. That the door was open. And that crossing it, in the end, was neither a good deal nor a feat, but only what someone does who has stopped kneeling before a tribunal that never had, over them, the authority they granted it.

Epilogue

This book does not contain, in its seventeen chapters, a single first person. It was a decision, and I think the right one: I wanted an argument, not a confession, something that stood on its logic and not on my biography. But a book has a right to one last page in another voice, and this is mine. Here I do speak.

It took me a while to realize something that now strikes me as obvious to the point of embarrassment: that writing this book was, itself, one of the acts the book describes. The most exposed of all, in fact. Publishing, finishing, putting a thesis into the world to be judged—I devoted a whole chapter to explaining that this is the toll of courage almost in its pure state, and I wrote it feeling, about these very pages, exactly the fear I was diagnosing in the abstract. I spent months arguing that the fear of judgment is a cage while inhabiting that cage completely, watching the cursor blink, wondering who I was to write this, imagining the verdict of readers who did not yet exist.

Theory and practice met in the writing, and I did not always come out of the encounter looking good.

Because that was the first thing I discovered, and it is not flattering. Understanding the arbitrage did not make me stop paying the tax. Knowing the alarm was miscalibrated did not make it sound any quieter. I wrote about the one who stays silent in the car and had to admit that I am, with enormous frequency, one of the twenty-nine. There are acts from this very catalog that I still avoid, emails I do not send, conversations I let pass, things I do not say. Knowing the mechanism of a cage, it turns out, does not get you out of it. Writing an entire book about the open door did not turn me into someone who always crosses it. It turned me into someone who, at least, can no longer pretend not to see it.

And there is the second thing I learned, which is more important and harder to accept. I did not come out of this book free. The very logic of what I wrote forbids me that tidy ending, the "and then I was liberated." The alarm does not switch off; I said so in the chapter on the tribe and I hold it with more conviction now that I have lived it by writing it. The only thing that changed, and it is not nothing, is that I stopped granting it the last word so often. Not with less fear. With less obedience. Freedom, if I can use that word for what is mine, was not a place I arrived at, but a practice I began, and continue, clumsily, every day. Each morning the door is there again. Each morning the toll of seconds is there again. And the work is not to become someone who no longer feels it, but someone who crosses it anyway, a little more often than yesterday.

I began writing this believing I was describing a pattern I had observed in others, a curiosity of human behavior that struck me as unjustly ignored. I ended up discovering that I was describing my own life: my own evasions, my own cowardly calculations disguised as prudence, my own slow and unfinished liberation. The book that was going to be about the world turned out to be a mirror. You sit down to explain a phenomenon and, if you are honest, at some point you lift your eyes from the page and recognize yourself in the diagnosis. Writing, when it is done in earnest, is not transferring to paper what you already knew; it is discovering, by force of having to sustain each sentence, what you did not know you knew, and sometimes what you did not want to know. This book changed me while I made it, and I suspect that is the only real proof that it was worth making.

I do not know whether I am freer than when I started. I know I see the bars better, mine, the ones I have left. And I have come to think that this is, perhaps, all the freedom available: not a condition conquered once and for all, but an evolution that does not end, a coming to see oneself with more clarity and yielding a little more ground to fear with each thing one dares to do. There is no final version of yourself waiting on the other side of the last page. There is only the process, which continues, and which if I am lucky will continue to the end, because the day I believe I have arrived will be the day I have gone back, without noticing, to sitting in silence in my own car.

If reading these pages did something for you, I suspect it was, in small, the same thing writing them did for me: not to give you a technique or an advantage, but to make your own cage, and your own door, a little more visible. What you do with that door is not the book's business. But now you see it. I wrote seventeen chapters, at bottom, in order to see it better. I am still learning to cross it.

On the Ideas in This Book

This book is not an academic work and carries no apparatus of citations. It argues in prose, and many of the notions it uses—loss aversion, survivorship bias, convexity, Goodhart's law—have become part of the common language of anyone who reads about decisions and behavior. Even so, those ideas have owners, and honesty asks that this be acknowledged. What follows is not a list of works cited, because the text does not cite them one by one; it is an acknowledgment of the sources behind its way of thinking, and an invitation to anyone who wants to go deeper than this essay.

On how the fear of losing weighs more than the hope of gaining, and on how badly we predict our own reactions and other people's, the reference is Daniel Kahneman and Amos Tversky, whose work on loss aversion and the biases of judgment underlies much of chapters four and five. An accessible entry point is Daniel Kahneman, *Thinking, Fast and Slow* (2011).

The idea of a convex profile—bounded loss, open gain—and the idea that certain exposures benefit from uncertainty instead of suffering it run through chapters five and seven. They are treated in depth in the work of Nassim Nicholas Taleb, in particular *Antifragile* (2012) and *The Black Swan* (2007).

The survivorship bias of chapter eleven—counting only those who made it and forgetting those who did not—has a concrete and elegant origin: the work of the statistician Abraham Wald during the Second World War, analyzing where to reinforce aircraft based, precisely, on the ones that had not come back.

Goodhart's law in chapter fourteen—when a measure becomes a target, it ceases to be a good measure—is due to the economist Charles Goodhart, and was formulated as an aphorism by the anthropologist Marilyn Strathern.

The moral argument of chapter sixteen leans on an old tradition. The idea that domination is sustained because the subjected lend their consent is Étienne de La Boétie's, in his *Discourse on Voluntary Servitude*, written around 1548. The notion that governing oneself is the root of dignity, and not one technique among others, has echoes running from autonomy in modern moral philosophy to the self-reliance of Ralph Waldo Emerson's essay.

For anyone who wants to keep pulling the thread, any of these works opens a different door into the same room this book tries to describe.

About the Author

Gabriel Toledo was born in Cali, Colombia, in 2006. He began writing this book believing it described other people, and ended up discovering it described himself. It is the first he has published.

www.ingramcontent.com/pod-product-compliance
Lightning Source LLC
LaVergne TN
LVHW100728061126
851857LV00011B/442
* 9 7 9 8 9 9 7 1 3 0 7 2 5 *